Agility

making innovation and change happen

Colin Ashurst

Contents

Preface

This book provides a framework for an approach to projects that is designed to enable innovation and the successful delivery of benefits from IT-enabled change. I have focused on IT-enabled change but the ideas are applicable to many types of projects.

I have drawn on two strands of theory and practice that have been evolving over the last 15 or more years. Firstly, benefits-driven approaches to projects that focus on identifying and delivering benefits for customers, employees and other stakeholders. Secondly, agile approaches that enable innovation and help a team of people work together effectively to realize the potential benefits.

In this book, I've brought these two perspectives together. I set out the principles, process and practices that underpin a successful approach to projects that reflects the challenges of a complex and fast changing business environment.

The framework set out in the book can very easily be adapted for many types of projects. In fact, it is really about *an agile way of life,* as for many of us working life is a series of projects both large and small.

I hope the framework and practices in this book can help you make a difference in your organization. I hope it will also help many organizations tackle the problems they face in innovation and delivering change. The key is to use the ideas. Have a go.

Acknowledgements

This book draws on many sources. The two key foundations are: firstly, Benefits Management[1]: developed by John Ward, Peter Murray and others at Cranfield Information Systems Research Centre and secondly, Microsoft Solutions Framework (Version 3) – developed by David Preedy, Allison Robins and others at Microsoft, which provides an excellent example of an agile approach to projects.

In addition, the practices and examples draw on my own practical experience over the last 30 years. Mostly it has been great fun. Even the times that were difficult have been great sources of learning. Thanks to the many people who have been friends and colleagues, and have helped me in the process of learning. I'd particularly like to thank Peter Murray for his friendship and guidance.

Most recently, I have worked extensively with Alison Freer (www.thinkfreer.com) who is now my co-director at Lead and Transform (www.leadandtransformit.com). Alison brings insight into people and expertise in leadership development that is of huge value. I think that in this first version of this book I am only just starting to reflect this. I hope to do better next time.

Note:

There is an important distinction to make between Information Systems (IS) and Information Technology (IT). For the moment, we are just using IT as a general term.

---

[1] See: Ward, J. and Daniel, E. (2006) *Benefits Management*. John Wiley & Sons also Ward J and Murray P (2000) *Benefits Management Best Practice Guidelines*. Information Systems Research Centre – Cranfield School of Management.

1   Benefits realization from IT: foundations

Key topics covered in this chapter:

- *The opportunities for organizations able to realize the strategic potential of IT through business innovation and transformation are significant.*

- *Benefits from IT come from using the technology to enable people to do things differently.*

- *Success in realizing benefits from IT requires a 'benefits mindset.' A number of guiding principles clarify key aspects of this mindset.*

- *Success in realizing benefits from IT depends on business leadership underpinned by multi-disciplinary teamwork.*

- *An organization needs to develop a set of competences to enable it to realize benefits from IT.*

- *We outline the need for a benefits 'toolkit' to provide a way to share practices contributing to effective teamwork and leadership. The toolkit helps to bring to life the organizational competences required to realize benefits from IT-enabled change.*

Realizing the strategic potential of IT?

Innovation in IT is continuing at a very rapid pace and will continue to provide new opportunities for organizations. IT has a critical role to play in the success of all sizes of organization from the one-person start-up to the very largest:

"I really think that the way companies implement business processes, organizational change, and IT-driven innovation is what differentiates the leaders from the laggers. Rather than leveling the playing field, IT is actually leading to greater discrepancies. In most industries the top companies are pulling further away from the companies in the middle and the bottom of the competitive spectrum."

Erik Brynjolfsson. MIT Sloan Management Review, Spring 2010

One of the factors that sets apart the leaders is their ability to realize benefits from IT-enabled change. This book provides a framework to help you and your organization succeed.

Rapid IT innovation: enabling business change and transformation

Technology has developed at an astounding speed. Around 15 years ago, a Terabyte of disk storage would have filled a large data centre and cost millions of pounds. Now you can have a 1Tb external drive plugged into your laptop for around £65, and the 2Tb memory stick is on its way. Similar developments have affected processor power and communication networks. As Bill Gates is reputed to have said, "If GM had kept up with technology like the computer industry has, we would all be driving $25 cars that got 1000 mpg."

Technology by itself is not the source of benefits. Benefits come when the technology is used to enable *people* to do things differently. Technology developments have enabled rapid innovation across all sectors of the economy, enabling new products, services and ways of working.

While we acknowledge that there can be a lot of hype about the extent and speed of change, continued, rapid innovation in technology is going to be a major driver of challenges and opportunities for organizations in the years ahead.

Pervasive impact of IT: opportunities for integration and efficiency

The improved price-performance of IT and the increasing power of software, often available on a pay-per-use basis over the Internet (Software as a Service / Cloud Computing), has made IT pervasive. There continue to be opportunities for cost savings from improved efficiency, and for improved effectiveness through integration within and between organizations. Newer trends, including collaborative technologies (e.g. Web 2.0), are changing customer expectations and bringing new opportunities for innovation.

IT critical to business success: further action needed to increase benefits realization

We carried out a survey between Dec 2009 and Feb 2010 to explore the views of senior business managers on the question: "have organizations got the leadership capabilities to realize the strategic potential of information systems?" Of the 117 responses, 55% were from Board level management and a total of 75% were from senior business and IT management.

The survey results suggest that Information Technology (IT) is critical to day-to-day operations and is a key contributor to current and future sources of competitive advantage (a total of 94% of 117 respondents). IT also makes an important contribution to cost reduction and improving efficiency (70% were satisfied or very satisfied).

IT risk is taken into consideration by senior management (69%). But, it is a concern that in only 27% of cases did senior management take action to obtain information on IT trends and new business opportunities enabled by IT. This contrasts with the strategic role of IT.

There was strong evidence of the barrier between business and IT: only 29% agreed or strongly agreed that senior business and IT managers speak the same language. So, even if there is some IT presence in the boardroom there is a broad problem of communication.

Based on all the responses, the responses from the survey indicate that senior management have expertise in IT strategy and project delivery (44%). The view from senior IT managers is less positive, in fact only 12% agree that senior business management have expertise in these areas. Only 26% agreed that leadership development activities currently address business manager engagement in IT strategy and project sponsorship. So there is also evidence of a need for action to develop skills in this area.

There are crucial issues here. IT is critical to business success, but there is only limited focus on future strategic opportunities. There is limited focus on developing the leadership capabilities required to realize the strategic potential of IT. Above all, there is a language barrier between senior business and IT management, which makes it hard to tackle any of the other issues.

This book is a contribution to tackling a number of these issues. Business managers do not need to develop the same specialist experience as their IT colleagues, but they do need the knowledge, skills and confidence to play significant roles in realizing benefits from IT investments effectively: they need to be 'IT savvy'. IT professionals need to be more 'business savvy' and to learn to speak the same language as their business colleagues.

This book is aimed at anyone who wants to help their team, department or organization realize the strategic potential of IT. It tackles the real-world challenges of succeeding with business innovation and change.

The benefits-driven approach provides a common language

The goal of this book is to help individuals and organizations succeed in realizing benefits from projects and programmes of IT-enabled change. It is built around a toolkit of practices for a benefits-driven approach to IT. It provides the basis for a common language, enabling the different players involved in these complex, challenging ventures to work together effectively in high performing, multi-disciplinary teams.

There are a number of reasons for starting here. Firstly, the perspective of individuals: projects are the right place to start to learn the ideas and practices of a benefits-driven approach. This is a concrete starting point, which is within the experience of many readers. Starting here provides a foundation for moving on to consider a benefits-driven approach to business strategy and management of the IT portfolio. Secondly, from an organizational perspective it is important to make improvements at this level by developing an enhanced ability to realize benefits from projects and programmes. Strategy discussions will progress more smoothly once the potential strategic contribution of IS/IT has been demonstrated and the credibility of the IT function is enhanced.

In the rest of this chapter, we develop foundations for the book. Firstly, we set out the need for a benefits-driven approach to investments in IT-enabled change. We introduce a number of principles for benefits realization, which guide our approach. Then we set out a framework for a benefits realization capability, which is the basis for exploring how to approach benefits realization from project, portfolio and organizational perspectives. Then we introduce the idea of 'practices', which underpin the benefits realization toolkit we present in later sections of the book.

From technology implementation to benefits realization

We carried out over 50 case studies in a wide range of sectors and locations. This research revealed a very substantial gap between what we *know* about the value of adopting a strong benefits focus when managing projects, and what happens in *practice*, where the focus is overwhelmingly on delivery of a technical solution. The vast majority of the projects investigated focused on the design and delivery of an IT solution, with only limited consideration of wider issues. There was no example of explicit adoption of a well-integrated portfolio of practices for benefits realization, which we could truthfully label a *benefits-driven* approach. It was also very interesting to see that organizations seemed content with the current situation. One project manager suggested that just to get the IT solution delivered to time, cost and quality goals would be a major achievement. When his project delivered, he said "*the customer was deeply moved when they saw that IT projects can be done like this*". Overall, delivery of an IT solution was seen as success, and project roles did not clearly address wider issues of benefits realization. This is the IT 'mindset' – that delivery of the technology means that the job is done.

Most organizations produce a business case before starting an investment in IT. Many think this means they are focusing on benefits. However, in most cases the business case is simply there to release the money and other resources, and is only very loosely linked to the activity of the project, which often becomes delivery of a technology solution.

The fundamental key to success, and reducing the reported 70+% failure rate of IT projects, is recognizing that the technology by itself is simply a cost (See Figure 1.1). The benefits come from *using* the technology to enable *people* to do things differently. Our benefits-driven approach focuses on these people – customers, employees and other stakeholders of the organization. We seek to identify very clearly, what the potential benefits are for these stakeholders and to focus the project on delivering them. In the framework set out in this book, we are making benefits realization the focus of activity from planning through delivery to exploitation. The focus is on benefits from start to finish: what are they and how do we bring them about.

Project Failure
Many studies have reported high project failure rates in terms of benefits realization. Often 70% or more of projects are seen as failing. The series of Chaos Reports from the Standish Group (www.standishgroup.com) are widely quoted. For example, www.cio.com quoted the 2009 report: "Specifically, 32 percent of IT projects were considered successful, having been completed on time, on budget and with the required features and functions. Nearly one-in-four (24 percent) IT projects were considered failures, having been cancelled before they were completed, or having been delivered but never used. The rest (44 percent) were considered challenged: They were finished late, over budget, or with fewer than the required features and functions."

There is room to question these figures. Are they measuring the right things at the right time? Did the organizations make sensible choices about which projects to invest in? The issue is not the precise failure rate. What we do know is that too many projects fail to deliver the intended and potential benefits.

This situation has not changed; in many senses, the challenge is getting greater as the focus shifts from automation to innovation and achieving more with fewer resources.

Figure 1.1: Exploring project failure

Principles for benefits realization

The shift of focus from technology implementation to benefits realization is the development of a benefits 'mindset.' Do people think and talk about benefits for stakeholders as opposed to technology features? Do they talk about what benefits the project will deliver then refuse to commit resources for the change management activities that will help realize the benefits?

The principles for benefits realization (Figure 1.2) draw on a number of sources and make aspects of the benefits 'mindset' more explicit. The principles provide important context for the details of the benefits-driven approach set out later in the book. If there are doubts about how to approach a specific situation, the principles are a valuable reference point.

1) Performance only improves when *people* do things differently.

The first principle makes the point that the technology itself is not the source of benefits. Benefits arise when *people* do things differently. It follows directly that the project needs to focus on the benefits for people (stakeholders), the new ways of working (what are they doing differently) and the changes required to bring about these new ways of working. We might continue to use 'IT project' as shorthand but really, we are talking about projects and programmes of IT-enabled business change.

This principle comes directly from the work of John Ward on Benefits Management – see Further Reading.

2) Motivated individuals and teams, with the environment and leadership they need, will deliver innovation and value.

We draw on the agile principles (see www.agilealliance.org) to emphasize the importance of motivated, empowered teams. The people involved are skilled, professional, knowledge workers. The challenges involved in benefits realization are complex. In all projects, and specifically when innovation is a goal, it is vital to focus on skills and enabling people to work together effectively in multi-disciplinary teams. This does not mean dispensing with discipline and control, but it does mean some traditional project management practices may not be helpful.

3) Focus on the delivery of value to customers and other stakeholders throughout the lifecycle.

Principle 3 builds on Principle 1 to emphasize that the benefits focus relates to customers and other stakeholders. The emphasis must continue through the lifecycle of the investment. The initial emphasis when exploring an opportunity is on benefits rather than technology implementation. The project itself becomes IT-enabled business change that tackles people, process and technology. Then the focus on benefits continues through the life of the 'assets' that have been developed.

4) Realization of benefits will depend on the participation of all relevant stakeholders.

The principle builds on Principle 2. Benefits realization depends on engagement with the stakeholders, and their active participation through the project. The practices required to engage key groups will vary, but the principle makes clear that the project scope is not delivering technology, but active participation of stakeholders to provide their insights and to bring about change.

5) Benefits arise when new capabilities are exploited and managed to the advantage of stakeholders.

The investment in IT-enabled change results in a new organizational capability: technology, processes, information, and people educated in using the information and systems. Benefits arise over an extended period, based on how these capabilities are exploited and managed. Typically, there is an extended process of learning as the new capabilities are explored, skills are developed, and the opportunities for the customer are discovered. This process needs to be actively managed or the capability will stagnate, remaining as it was when the systems went live and the changes first introduced.

Succeeding with investments in IT - principles for a benefits-driven approach

1. Performance only improves when people do things differently.

2. Motivated individuals and teams, with the environment and leadership they need, will deliver innovation and value.

3. Focus on the delivery of value to customers and other stakeholders throughout the lifecycle.

4. Realization of benefits will depend on the participation of all relevant stakeholders.

5. Benefits arise when new capabilities are exploited and managed to the advantage of stakeholders.

6. Exploitation of the potential of IT requires a major form of organizational and individual learning.

The principles draw on work by the Agile Alliance, Chris Clegg, Ken Eason, David Preedy and the Microsoft Solutions Framework team, and John Ward.

Figure 1.2: Principles for a benefits-driven approach

6) Exploitation of the potential of IT requires a major form of organizational and individual learning.

This principle is closely related to #5. It has particular relevance to our focus on benefits from innovation. It makes the crucial point that this is not a simple linear process: define requirements – design and implement a system – realize benefits. The strategic potential of IT is realized through a much more complex process of organizational learning and change.

We can still set some requirements, but we take a phased, incremental approach because we know that during a project we are likely to discover new possibilities, which we can capture through further phases of change, which in turn will lead to new learning.

Overall, the principles encapsulate a benefits 'mindset' which provides a crucial foundation for a benefits-driven approach to be successfully adopted.

Benefits realization capability – a framework

The idea of a 'benefits realization capability' is particularly relevant to the challenge of benefits realization from investments in IT, as it facilitates exploration of the organization as a whole and not just the IT function. In this book, we are making use of a model of the organizational competences that contribute to this benefits realization capability.

We use the following definitions:

Benefits realization...

Delivering value to customers and other stakeholders, and improving organizational performance through benefits-driven programmes and projects of IT-enabled change.

Benefits realization capability...

The organization-wide capability to consistently realize value from investments in IT-enabled change and transformation.

The benefits realization capability of an organization, comprises four distinct, yet highly inter-related competences (Figure 1.3).

Benefits Planning: benefits do not simply emerge, as if by magic, from the introduction of a new technology, their realization needs to be carefully planned and managed from the very beginning of thinking about any investment in change. Benefits Planning includes a strategic perspective, enabling innovation and deciding which projects to undertake, as well as benefits-focused planning of individual projects.

Benefits Delivery: benefits primarily arise from the organizational change that accompanies an IT implementation, rather than directly from the technology itself. The benefits and related changes need to be the focus of activity.

Benefits Review: organizations must monitor and evaluate results on an on-going basis. This will improve the results of individual projects, and ensure that the organization's ability to deliver business value improves over time.

Benefits Exploitation: the quest to leverage benefits from business software should not cease as soon as it has been implemented. Continued focus is required over the life of the investment.

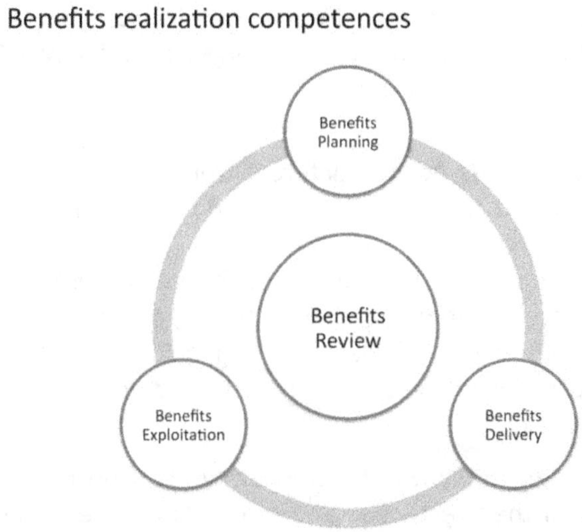

Benefits realization competences

Figure 1.3: Organizational competences for benefits realization

Competences have both explicit and tacit elements and can be hard for managers to deal with. One way of bringing a competence to life is through adoption of a *toolkit* of *practices*, each of which can be tailored to the needs and circumstances of a specific organization. The concept of a 'practice' is a way to capture and communicate 'what works', how to get things done.

Developing effective practice: the benefits realization toolkit

What did you do at work today? Perhaps there was a meeting, perhaps quite a number of them. Some emails, phone calls and interruptions from people passing by. Did you write a report, a presentation, or a progress report? Did you spend time helping, advising or reviewing the progress of others?

How effective were you? What did you achieve? What obstacles got in your way?

Were you more effective than last week or last year? Did you put into practice what you had learned from your colleagues, from the last course or educational programme, to work more effectively?

Improving effectiveness?

For most of us, one day is not too different from the next, even if you are in a varied and challenging role. We do similar things and we use a core set of routines – a personal 'toolkit' to tackle what we do day-to-day. For example, we approach planning a meeting or preparing a presentation in much the same way. Many successful managers work this way and can quickly explain the structure they use for a presentation, proposal or how they approach other activities.

This toolkit only changes slowly. Even when we change roles and employers, many of these activities and the tools we use to tackle them stay the same. Often the formal processes and procedures of the organization have only a limited impact on what we do – we operate based on our experience and perhaps our professional education within our specific discipline.

Does effectiveness matter?

In many of the scenarios that we face day to day and that are at the core of our roles as professionals and knowledge workers there are huge variations in the effectiveness of individuals. You will know who runs meetings effectively in your organization, for example.

Research into the productivity of software developers highlighted a 10:1 difference in productivity between the best and the worst individuals and teams. That is a big difference – and it wasn't due to seniority, years of experience or technology. There are probably similar, very large differences in other knowledge work scenarios.

So, what do you do if you are a manager and you want to improve the performance of your team, department or organization? What do you do if you want to improve your own effectiveness?

How can we improve the effectiveness of individuals and teams?

There is a view that being effective, or a good leader for example, depends on intangible, tacit skills, and it is not possible to make them explicit. There might be some element of truth in that. But does that mean we can do nothing to improve performance? No. Tacit skills could be articulated readily if organizational members were simply asked the question "how do you do that?" Very often, we can capture, or codify, important elements that lead to effectiveness and share them. The tension between codifying nothing, thereby risking the loss of important information, and trying to codify everything, risking banality, is at the very core of attempts at knowledge management. There is an 'optimal amount of structure' and if knowledge is to remain useful once made explicit, a link with the context in which the knowledge was used, and thus in which it might be reused, must be retained.

The challenge is to tackle problems by cutting them up into chunks that can be analyzed, understood and handled. This is a key strategy of successful managers – they are able to tackle a wide variety of problems by improvising and making use of relevant techniques from their 'toolkit'. So, improving performance requires extending the toolkit, getting better at using the tools in it effectively, and learning how to break problems down so that they can be tackled with the tools we have available.

A new approach to improving effectiveness

Some of us formalize our 'toolkit' with a collection of templates and a record of ideas of how to tackle common activities, so that we avoid reinventing the wheel, for example, each time we want to plan a meeting, facilitate a workshop or conduct an interview. This approach can help us maintain and extend our knowledge over time. It turns out to be an effective approach to learning and knowledge management and is a good way to improve our own efficiency and effectiveness and to share ideas or provide advice to others.

To improve effectiveness it makes sense to go 'with the grain' of how people think and work. What if we try and build on this idea of a personal toolkit? What if we find a consistent structure and make it a collaborative activity so that we have a shared toolkit connecting people so that they can think together, enabling individual and group learning and bringing together different people with different experiences, allowing them to contribute their knowledge in a team.

The benefits realization toolkit

The benefits realization toolkit builds on these ideas. The toolkit is a collection of techniques that can be used during a project. We have introduced a number of the tools in this book, for example 'stakeholder analysis.'

The toolkit is different from a 'methodology.' It addresses people and teamwork as well as the more process oriented aspects of a project (for example risk management). By using 'toolkit' we aim to highlight that *when* and *how* to use the tools is up to the project team. The tools are there to help them achieve their goals. Many of the tools are very simple. Success depends on using them effectively, which requires experience.

The toolkit provides a basis for a shared language and a way of working that enables business and IT leaders, and multi-disciplinary teams engaged in realizing benefits from IT-enabled change, to work together effectively. In the book, we present key elements of the toolkit in the context of a framework for a benefits-driven project. In practice, individuals, teams and organizations will build expertise in using the tools and learn to adapt them as they apply them in a range of situations.

The toolkit...

The example 'round tables' (Figure 1.4) shows how the 'tools' can be documented. It comes from guidelines we developed with participants at a series of workshops.

The simple example was one of a number used to document agreed ways of working for a networking group bringing together business and academic participants.

Round tables

Forum meetings are held at round tables to encourage discussion

We want to develop an atmosphere of learning from each other. This means that the speakers must not dominate the sessions and that there must be opportunities for interaction in small groups and across all the attendees.

***

Traditional programmes tend to line up their students in large tiered lecture theatres so that they can focus on the speakers. By contrast, in the Forum we will restrict numbers in order to maximize debate.

We will be seated café-style, at round tables in order to enable engagement in immediate and deep discussion whenever an opportunity presents itself. This layout encourages fast and efficient interaction to take place within and across table groups.

***

The round tables, by themselves are not sufficient to ensure that we have participative sessions. We will also rely on the **50:50 rule, learning by doing** and the **variety of meetings** to encourage discussion, debate and learning from each other.

Figure 1.4: A simple example of the patterns format for capturing and sharing knowledge

The toolkit is built on the ideas of practices and patterns. The structure provides a link with the specific context(s) in which the knowledge is useful. In addition to the 'solution' (recommendation for action to improve the problematic situation), a rationale is provided to give insight into the complexities of the situation and the reasons the solution works. Rationale and context are vital so that users have the understanding to adapt and improvise as they apply the knowledge in their situation.

In the round tables example we adopted the following structure:

- **Name**: the name seeks to capture the essence of the pattern.

- **Summary** (often with picture): support the name and try to reinforce the understanding of the pattern

- **Context**: a brief statement that indicates the context and relevance of the pattern.

***

- **Rationale** – explains the different forces involved in the problematic situation and how the solution responds to these forces. In these examples, this section is kept brief. The proposed **solution** is in bold.

***

- **Links** are given to related patterns.

The benefits toolkit – in this book

In this book we describe *core* elements of the benefits toolkit in some detail and outline a number of additional tools. Core tools are highlight by a [T] in the relevant section heading. The Appendix provides more information on the toolkit and summarises the main tools in relation to the stages of the project lifecycle.

This approach can be used to capture and share knowledge in many situations.

In summary: the contribution of this book

Being able to realize the strategic potential of IT to deliver value to customers and other stakeholders, and to improve organizational performance is a crucial issue for every organization. The challenge is simply to achieve the benefits, get value for money, and avoid the risk of failure – in an environment where the technology, customer expectations and the business environment are changing rapidly!

There is a need for vision and leadership. The need for effective leadership of business transformation is greater than ever before. While we have much less money to spend, we must do it much more effectively. We must also put much more effort into exploiting the potential of all the investments in IT we have made in the past. In many organizations the potential of the IT systems and the information they provide is seriously underexploited – we need to focus on nurturing and realizing the potential of these significant organizational assets.

The core issues of benefits realization are the same regardless of the size or sector of the organization. These are business issues and this book is aimed at building a common language between professionals from business and IT. We want to see business savvy IT professionals and IT savvy business leaders.

In this book, we introduce a framework for managing an IT project and then explore key aspects of a benefits-driven approach at each stage of the project lifecycle. We then consider specific issues of enabling innovation and steps to develop a benefits-driven approach to projects and programmes within an organization.

***

2 The e^{4+1} project framework

Key topics covered in this chapter:

- *We introduce the e^{4+1} framework, which provides a flexible framework for a wide range of projects. It can be adopted for a specific project or the complete portfolio of projects within an organization.*

- *The e^{4+1} framework is underpinned by a number of key principles and practices. The benefits toolkit provides guidance on the specific practices.*

- *The e^{4+1} framework is designed to be adaptable to a range of scenarios and to be a good fit when business innovation and transformation is the goal.*

- *The e^{4+1} framework tackles the entire investment lifecycle from idea through to exploitation of the resulting information, systems and processes. It provides specific milestones and deliverables that enable effective cross-project communication and sharing of good practices.*

Features of the e^{4+1} project framework

In this chapter, we introduce the **e^{4+1}** project framework. It draws on experience of both traditional approaches to projects, such as PRINCE2, and 'agile' approaches that have their roots in software development and design. **e^{4+1}** has a number of specific features:

Firstly, it focuses on people throughout the lifecycle recognizing that success comes from motivated, effective multi-disciplinary teams and that project processes should be designed primarily to help the team and their stakeholder's work effectively to deliver benefits.

Secondly, **e^{4+1}** takes the view that a project starts from the initial idea. The goal is to bring focus and momentum from this early stage, rather than the traditional starting point, often months or years later, when the idea has been developed into a business case and project plan. This early focus and momentum is crucial in a fast-moving business environment and for managing the allocation of scarce organizational resources to the highest value ideas.

e^{4+1} also continues beyond the traditional end-point of projects. Most projects end soon after the cutover to the new systems and processes. In **e^{4+1}** we take the view that benefits are only realized from the new ways of working that result from the cutover and that these take time to bed in and develop. In many situations, crucial learning about the benefits and how to realize them takes place at this stage and the project team need to continue their focus on benefits at this stage so we go beyond e^4 to **e^{4+1}** with the final 'Expand' stage.

e^{4+1} has an explicit focus on benefits for stakeholders rather than the delivery or procurement of software.

Finally, **e^{4+1}** reflects our view that there are serious flaws in the assumptions underlying traditional approaches to projects. Especially in scenarios where innovation is the goal, the approach to a project has to enable significant learning about what is possible and what is beneficial for the stakeholders during the life of the project. Innovative projects have to enable adaptation and change and they have to establish a simple, effective framework of management and control that does not stifle innovation and progress with bureaucracy. To put it bluntly, the traditional model, in which you define in detail *exactly* what the outcomes will be before you start a project, is nonsense if the goal is business innovation.

In this chapter we start by outlining the value of a project framework, then set out some fundamental principles that underpin e^{4+1}, then we set out the different stages of e^{4+1}. Finally, we put the framework in context of other methods and summarize its value in enabling benefits realization from IT-enabled business innovation.

The value of a project framework

In our view a project framework is different from a project method or methodology in important ways. It has a number of important elements: guiding principles that make clear important views about what leads to success; a clear framework for the project lifecycle, breaking it down into specific stages with defined deliverables; and specific practices or tools that can be adopted at different stages. It is not prescriptive. The framework provides guidance for teams to help them work effectively. A project framework has considerable value for an individual project and for the organization managing a diverse portfolio of projects.

For a specific project the framework breaks the project down into a number of clear stages each with specific deliverables. This should help the project team be clear about their roles and the focus of their activities at any particular stage. It also helps the team communicate with management and other stakeholders. The split of the project into a number of clear stages, none of which is more than a few weeks in duration, also provides focus and motivation for the team. Innovation often brings many options and much uncertainty, the focus on short-term goals balances space to innovate with a drive for closure and progress.

At the organizational level there are many additional benefits of adopting a consistent framework for projects. A consistent approach helps management control the entire portfolio of investments and enables groups that have to be involved in many projects (for example, IT infrastructure and security) to engage effectively at the right time. A consistent framework also provides a basis for sharing learning between projects and avoids 'reinventing the wheel' in areas that do not add a great deal of value ('how should we format the progress report on this project?'). Practices can be reused at many levels; for example, a communications strategy addressing how to engage with the diverse groups in a professional organization, or a document setting out team structure and roles, or perhaps a web-based environment and set of templates for team collaboration and stakeholder engagement. This shared learning increases effectiveness by communicating good ideas and increases efficiency by avoiding time consuming duplication of effort. Perhaps most importantly, the shared framework and practices help the rapid formation of effective teams as projects are established and as people move from project to project.

Fundamentals

In this section we outline a number of fundamental principles and practices that underpin e^{4+1}.

Benefits focus throughout the lifecycle

The 'benefits mindset' is the fundamental foundation for e^{4+1} and for any approach to benefits realization from IT-enabled change. The starting point is to consider 'what benefits can we deliver for stakeholders?' and NOT 'what software and technology features are required?' We certainly want to consider the technology and to do that from the early stages of the project as we consider what is possible. However, we shift our focus to benefits and new ways of working which are *enabled* by the technology and wider organizational changes.

The focus on benefits continues throughout the project lifecycle and the subsequent lifetime of the 'assets', the new technology and business processes (or new business service) that have resulted from the investment.

Classic objections to a benefits-driven approach are 'we have a robust business case' and perhaps 'we've already taken the savings out of the departmental budgets.' A benefits-driven approach is much more than a robust business case: it's about a focus on delivering value for stakeholders (not just cutting budgets); the changes that will result in the benefits; and the ownership of both the benefits and the related changes.

While it is important to have a clear understanding of the problematic situation to be tackled or the vision for the project, the focus on the precise definition of outcomes in the business case before the project starts is an illustration of the flawed thinking that will stifle innovation. We need a more truly commercial approach, which reflects the vision of the entrepreneur.

Engaged people realize benefits

At the heart of the approach is a focus on people. The emphasis is on people rather than process. In part this is an attempt to counteract the traditional focus on process over people, which underplays the role of committed individuals and effective teams in successful benefits realization. The focus on people affects all aspects of the project:

- The leadership of the sponsor and project management.
- The importance of effective teamwork and creating an environment where the team can work effectively.
- The importance of effective engagement of customers and other stakeholders.

The foundation for this emphasis is not a desire to create a 'nice' working environment or to keep people happy. It is recognition that empowered individuals and effective teamwork are key contributors to a successful project. Research published in Peopleware (DeMarco and Lister, 1999) indicates that there is a staggering 10:1 productivity difference between developers and development teams. The factors contributing to this difference are largely due to:

- the creation of an effective working environment – where the team can work together in one place.
- providing the freedom for individuals to take responsibility for their work.
- developing an effective team.

From a very different perspective we can view IT projects and software development as 'knowledge-intensive' activities. They certainly involve a range of professions and disciplines who have to work together in multi-disciplinary teams. Practices (represented by the toolkit for benefits realization), are valuable in sharing knowledge and establishing a 'common language.' They provide a framework for enabling the effective multi-disciplinary working required for IT-enabled change.

We emphasize key principles and a simple set of practices to help to build a common language and approach in these multi-disciplinary teams. The aim is to create an environment where skilled, professional workers can succeed, rather than to attempt to improve performance by imposing a detailed process and tight controls.

Phase benefits delivery

In practice a traditional 'waterfall' approach to projects often results in large, long projects as the team attempts to deliver all possible user requirements. For very good reasons the agile approach breaks away from this 'one shot' approach to change.

Agile projects keep teams small, have short durations (no longer than 6-9 months, and shorter where possible) and deliver the business solution (benefits) in phases over a series of these short projects or 'versioned releases'.

The first benefit of this approach is that smaller, shorter projects are much easier to manage and control. The risks are substantially lower than on larger projects. Complexity increases exponentially with the scale of the project. The shorter project also means that benefits are realized earlier.

Phase benefits delivery
incremental delivery of benefits

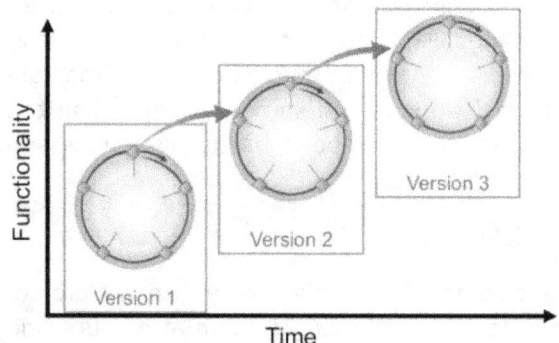

Minimize risks by breaking large projects into multiple versions. Reduce
time to realization of benefits

Figure 2.1: Phase benefits delivery

In addition, small teams tend to be more innovative and the short timescales are likely to result in greater motivation and stronger ownership.

A further benefit, which is crucial, is that delivery over a series of releases provides an opportunity for organizational learning. In scenarios of significant change and innovation, it allows the organization and customers to learn more about the potential benefits and how to realize them.

Milestone based control

Management focus should be on the major milestones (stage ends) determined by the project lifecycle. If the project is kept short (as it should be) this will typically provide a major review point every 4-8 weeks, which provides a motivating target for the project team, and reduces the risk of slippage between milestones for the sponsor and project board.

The deliverables at each milestone should be clearly defined. In some organizations a standard lifecycle is defined with the same stages and major deliverables for each project.

Benefits driven trade-offs

Project plans essentially balance resources (including costs), the project timescale and the 'features' being delivered. The business case provides a basis for assessing this against the potential benefits. Plans are without exception based on incomplete information, which is subject to uncertainty. As the project progresses the project team, project manager, project sponsor and project board will have to make decisions as new information arises.

The concept of making 'benefits driven trade-offs' is that as part of initial project planning there should be a clear decision on how decisions will be made as new information becomes available; for example, new requirements, more accurate estimates, or evidence of the productivity of the project team. For most projects the right approach is to fix the team size, set a target delivery date and then adjust the features delivered, if necessary, as new information arises. The delivery of benefits provides an overall context for these decisions and fits closely with the phasing of benefits delivery.

Enable innovation and learning

The traditional, waterfall model of the project lifecycle was based on the importance of getting the planning and design 'right' at the start of the project and then strictly controlling (preventing) change. This thinking is flawed, particularly if the scenario involves innovation.

The e^{4+1} lifecycle reflects the principles of an agile approach 'responding to change over following a plan.' The requirements and design emerge from the project process because of learning and the innovative ways of working of the team. The basis for this adaptive lifecycle is the spiral model of a project. The concept is that even within a single project or release the team cycle round the spiral of design, develop, and test a number of times. This builds on the use of prototypes that is emphasized as a key element of 'design thinking'. (See Further Reading.)

The e^{4+1} model provides a very effective framework for projects. It balances freedom and flexibility with tight control by focusing on regular milestones and specific deliverables.

The framework in outline

In this section, we provide an initial outline of key elements of the e^{4+1} framework. In later chapters we work through each stage in more detail exploring specific benefits-driven practices.

e^{4+1} project framework

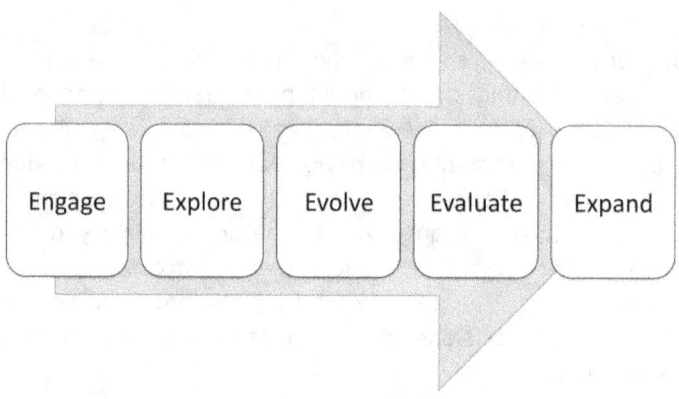

Figure 2.2: Outline of the e^{4+1} project framework

Engage

There are always so many ideas. Too many opportunities to invest time and resource into every one. How do you decide where to focus? How can you know at the start what the possibilities are?

Of course in many cases you can't know. In scenarios involving innovation, perhaps exploiting new technology, or just trying an idea learnt from elsewhere that is new to the organization, you just cannot be sure of the potential benefits. What will the customers really think? Can we adopt an idea that has worked well in another organization? The traditional approach based on the business plan, detailed planning and requirements documented and signed off up front, brings a perception of certainty and control, but the high failure rate of projects confirms that reality is different.

Engage is the start of a process of exploration and learning. It is the start of a series of small steps to discover and create possibilities, and to gradually focus on good ideas that have real potential for stakeholders and the organization.

Engage should be a rapid stage. The goal is to outline the opportunity by identifying and bringing together a group of the key stakeholders who would need to be involved in further steps. The output is a brief outline of the opportunity (a single page 'concept' document perhaps) and agreement whether to proceed further.

Explore

Explore builds on the rapid initial work done during Engage to establish a clear and agreed vision for the project and a benefits realization plan. The emphasis on learning and stakeholder engagement continues to be vital at this stage. The vision helps establish the broad goals for the project based on the contribution to the strategic objectives of the organization and the potential benefits to stakeholders.

The *benefits realization plan* is the critical deliverable from this stage. It brings together an agreed statement of:

- What the benefits are.

- How they will be measured.

- Who is responsible for delivering them (and when).

- What changes are required to realize them.

The *solution concept* is also vital. It provides an initial view of the solution in both business and technical terms. In many cases early prototyping will have been important in exploring what works to provide benefits for the different stakeholders.

The completion of the Explore stage is a second major project milestone and 'go / no-go' decision point. If innovation is an important driver, it is important to take some risks and explore different opportunities. As a result, not every project is successful and it is good practice to stop some projects at this point.

Evolve

The project team will be mobilized at this point if this has not started earlier. Alongside starting to build an effective team, a key challenge is to ensure the team have a clear understanding of the vision for the project that has been established in previous phases, and that there is commitment to delivering the intended benefits.

Evolve will usually be a major stage and it will often be subdivided into a number of smaller stages. Following an agile software development approach, Evolve will be split based on incremental delivery of elements of the underlying technical solution. In any case, it will often be useful to have a number of sub-stages to provide short-term goals and to enable regular reflection and learning. In many cases the solution and related benefit realization plan will continue to evolve as the project continues. Typically, there will be a 'phased freeze' as elements of the solution and plan are brought under change control (Figure 2.3).

Phased Freeze

The architect developed a conceptual design for the building, which gained enthusiastic approval. This provided a basis for starting work – by digging the foundations. Later on, the steelwork was put in place providing a skeleton to build on. Only much later on did the details emerge – of the layout of each floor, of lighting, colours and furnishings. With the right skills in the team, an IT system design emerges in a similar way. Technology infrastructure and core database design are 'baselined' early. Details of user interface can follow much later: the 'phased freeze' balances maintaining flexibility and achieving progress.

Figure 2.3: Phased freeze

Evaluate

Major and interim project milestones provide important opportunities for review and reflection. Evaluate is the key opportunity for a Benefits Review to consider:

- What benefits have been realized?

- What action is required to sustain and develop these benefits?

- Is there a way to deliver any planned benefits that have not yet been realized?

- Have there been any unexpected benefits and how can these be developed further?

- What learning is there for future projects and the wider organization?

Although conceptually simple, the challenge is to ensure that evaluation happens and that an environment is created where genuine learning can occur. The review needs to take place soon after implementation: but not too soon, there needs to be time for a benefits perspective to be possible, avoiding a focus on technical issues relating to 'going live.'

Expand

The framework is e^{4+1} not e^5 to emphasize Expand and to show that it is different from the other stages. Expand is the stage after a traditional perspective would say the project is complete. This 'post-live' period is crucial to the project and it is vital to continue the focus on benefits realization. Expand can be considered as ongoing management of the production service. The value of Expand for benefits realization means that it is important to include it as part of the project framework.

Preparations for Expand will have taken place throughout the project, specifically the activities relating to stakeholder engagement. During this stage, responsibilities will usually be handed over from the project team to operational management

The framework in context

e^{4+1} provides a fresh perspective on projects that is valuable for both newcomers to the world of project management and experienced project managers. We hope it will help organizations succeed with innovation and make engagement in projects more rewarding and fun for individuals. It is intended as an overall framework, including a set of principles and practices that can be adopted in many situations and adapted to reflect the specific opportunities and challenges of each situation.

There are many other approaches to projects, many with substantial backing from professional bodies and other groups. However, many organizations have no overall project framework and in many cases each project manager has to start from scratch in determining how to plan and manage a project. e^{4+1} can provide considerable value for an individual project or across an entire portfolio of projects. It brings the flexibility for learning and adaptation that is absent in traditional approaches. It brings a focus on specific milestones and deliverables.

e^{4+1} is most closely aligned with agile approaches to projects, but brings a focus on benefits from IT-enabled change rather than software delivery. It does not attempt to tackle the technical issues of software development and engineering. Most importantly, as with agile approaches, e^{4+1} focuses on people and sees process primarily as a way to enable multi-disciplinary teams to work effectively to deliver benefits from innovation.

We hope individuals and organizations will use e^{4+1}. Firstly, it can be used as a framework for projects small or large wherever they are found in organizations. Secondly, and perhaps most importantly, it is designed to reflect a new way of thinking about projects and how to succeed with benefits realization from projects and specifically investments in IT-enabled change. In this sense it highlights key principles and practices, which will be valuable irrespective of the explicit adoption of the framework. Finally, it can be used as a way of adapting and enhancing whatever approach to projects is currently in place within an organization.

Using e^{4+1} with other project frameworks

Many organizations do not use a specific project lifecycle. Even in large organizations the structure of the project is left to the project manager. Where organizations have adopted a specific method, such as PRINCE2, the specific lifecycle stages and deliverables are often not consistent across different projects.

In our view there is a lot of value for individual teams and for the organization as a whole to adopt a project framework that provides a common understanding of stages and deliverables. e^{4+1} provides a good option.

Where an existing approach is well established, we suggest you take the best of e^{4+1} to add to what is currently working well. Engage and Expand will rarely be in place. Also the principles and specific tools can be adapted and adopted to fit with a wide range of methods.

It is important to note that that the *principles* underpinning e^{4+1} may be significantly different from existing ways of working. Understanding and change at this level is probably more important than simply adopting new tools.

In summary

In this chapter we have introduced the e^{4+1} project framework. Drawing on our experience, we have designed the framework to offer a number of advantages over both traditional and agile approaches to projects:

- It focuses on people throughout the lifecycle recognizing that success comes from motivated, effective multi-disciplinary teams and effective stakeholder engagement.

- There is a focus on benefits for stakeholders throughout the lifecycle.

- We take the view that a project starts from the initial idea. The goal is to bring focus and momentum from this early stage. In many cases there is an opportunity to save months of time and effort.

- In e^{4+1} we take the view that benefits are only realized from new ways of working and that these take time to bed in and develop. In many situations crucial learning about the benefits and how to realize them takes place at this stage and the project team continue their focus on benefits at this stage.

Most importantly, e^{4+1} is designed to enable innovation.

***

3   Making a start: Engage

Key topics covered in this chapter:

o   *The Engage stage brings focus and momentum to a project from the initial identification of an opportunity.*

o   *Promising ideas are explored by a small initial group of stakeholders using two valuable elements of the benefits toolkit.*

o   *Stakeholder Expectations analysis provides insights into the potential benefits for customers and other relevant stakeholders.*

o   *The IT and Change Portfolio helps explore the strategic alignment and potential strategic contribution of the opportunity.*

o   *For valuable opportunities a short concept paper (a single page) is developed to capture the proposal and move forward to the Explore stage.*

Focus on benefits from day 1

Engage is a rapid first stage to turn an idea into the initial outline of an opportunity, which has the support of a key group of stakeholders. It also provides a way to filter out ideas that are not worth investigating further, or at least not at the moment.

Ideas can come from many sources, it is important to create an environment where ideas are encouraged, treated seriously and decision-makers are open to new opportunities. We consider the importance of generating ideas and explore ways of thinking about business value from IT that help assess an idea. We then explore two important practices that underpin activity at this stage:

- Stakeholder Expectations analysis: a valuable way to start with a focus on the customer and other stakeholders.

- The IT and Change portfolio: which helps determine priorities based on the alignment with the strategic objectives of the organization.

Sources of value from IT

IT makes different contributions to organizational performance in different organizations. The opportunities for realizing value depend on the strategy, structure and culture of the organization. Many different frameworks can be used to classify the different sources of value from IT.

We have taken a straightforward model to help consider the different sources of value from IT, as it provides helpful insights when considering real-world situations (Figure 3.1)

Many early IT investments were made to automate activities (payroll calculation, accounts payable, etc). Increasingly IT is being used in scenarios where the value comes from informating, embedding or communicating. In any scenario, it is important to consider which of these sources of value are relevant and to explore if there are benefits in other areas that have not initially been considered.

Sources of value from IT

Automate: substituting technology for labour

Informate: Complementing human information processing capabilities

Embed: replacing and enhancing mechanical and electro-mechanical controls

Communicate / collaborate: enhancing information sharing capabilities

Source: Cash, et al. (1994), Building the Information Age Organization - building on Zuboff (1988); In the Age of the Smart Machine

An example - sources of value from IT

Automate: matching of invoices, orders and goods received notes by an accounts payable system; payroll processing.

Informate: a business scorecard reporting system that provides managers with access to top level performance indicators and the ability to 'drill down' to see more information about any trends / changes.

Embed: the car that alerts the driver that it needs a service.

Communicate / collaborate: a worldwide virtual team in a consulting organization – asking for and sharing advice by using an email discussion group and an intranet site for sharing valuable documents and other resources.

Figure 3.1: Sources of value from IT

Insight and innovation

Ideas, insights and awareness of the problems that provide opportunities for innovation are all around us. Most people are full of ideas and are keen to act on them if they are given half a chance. It is only in unhealthy organizations that people just accept the current situation, however ineffective and inefficient it is.

Some ideas will come top-down from senior management as part of a strategic planning process. Many others will come from staff, customers, partners and competitors if we keep our eyes and ears open and we encourage people to share the ideas and insights they have.

There may also be opportunities to go out and search for ideas – perhaps at relevant conferences, online, or by specifically working to build up a network of relationships with individuals who may provide valuable ideas.

Taking time to develop an understanding of the business potential of new technologies is also important. This might involve investing time researching online and developing relationships with technical specialists internally as well as key vendors.

Many individuals and organizations have become risk averse because of previous bad experiences; for example, by being taken in by vendor hype about a new technology or by the failure of a major project. Given the pace of technology and business innovation most organizations can no longer take this approach and simply follow and wait. A much better approach is to take some risks and learn from experience. The key is to ensure that the risks are limited and that a new project does not put the future of the business at risk.

Figure 3.2 shows aspects of this complex web of ideas and relationships.

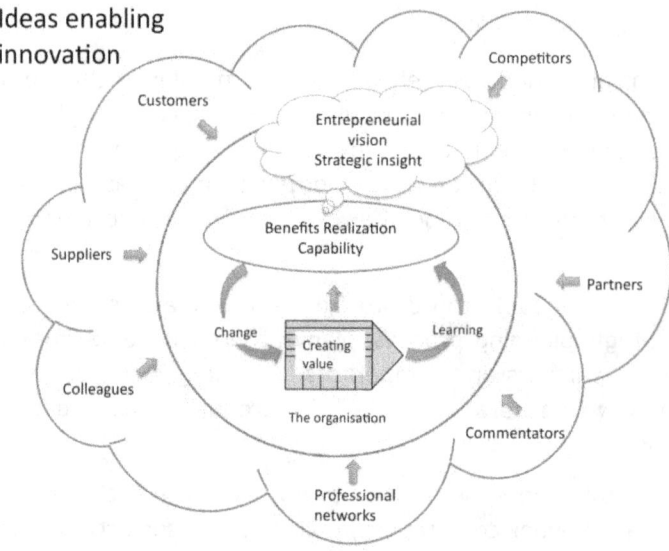

Figure 3.2: Ideas enabling innovation

Ideas come from everywhere, both inside and outside the organization. A key element of the benefits realization capability of the organization is the openness to ideas and the insight, vision and alertness to explore potentially valuable opportunities.

Stakeholder Expectations Analysis[T]: start with a focus on benefits for stakeholders

It is important to start a project with a clear perspective on how to create value for customers and other stakeholders (Figure 3.3). This counters the organizational perspective, which can often be reduced to 'make money'. While this is valid, perhaps translated into being 'cost effective' outside the private sector, it is does not tell us 'how.' The key to understanding 'how' is to start with a focus on benefits for stakeholders.

Stakeholder(s)

An individual or group of people who will benefit from the investment or are either directly or indirectly involved in making or are affected by the changes needed to realize the benefits.

See: Ward and Daniel (2006) Benefits Management

Figure 3.3 Stakeholder – a definition

One powerful technique, **Stakeholder Expectations Analysis**, is to brainstorm the expectations of each stakeholder group. It is usually part of a workshop session with a small group involved in exploring or identifying opportunities. There are two stages: first, identify relevant stakeholders and stakeholder groups. Some judgment is involved to determine relevant stakeholders and to decide how to segment stakeholders. For example, in the University, we would virtually always consider students as a number of groups; undergraduate, postgraduate taught, MBA, post-graduate research, executive. The second stage is to brainstorm the expectations or potential expectations of each stakeholder. We have found this works very effectively if captured directly on a PowerPoint slide as part of a workshop session. Each expectation can then be categorized for example:

- Critical: project will fail if this expectation is not met.

- Important: significant expectation, but project can succeed if it is not met.

- Preferred: would be very nice if this expectation could be met.

- Defer: although this is an expectation, the project will not seek to meet it and action should be considered to reduce the expectation.

- New: the stakeholder does not currently see the opportunity and work is required to get them to see the potential benefits.

We can use the Stakeholder Expectations model with a small group of people. At this early stage, it may reveal some gaps in our knowledge, which is fine as we can deal with that later if we proceed with work to turn the idea into a project. We can also decide later how to validate our understanding of the expectations of different stakeholders.

You can add to the process by thinking about your expectations of the stakeholder, its particularly relevant for partners and suppliers, but is useful for other groups as well. The opportunities come from creating new expectations or meeting critical / important expectations where there is currently a gap or a problem with the current product / or service. Although very straightforward, the practice provides a valuable way to get fresh insights into a situation. It allows you to look beyond current products, services and structures.

We can use the approach in at least two ways. One starting point would be to use it to develop ideas – by just taking a very open view of the situation and exploring expectations that are not being met. This could result in various opportunities for making improvements, or doing new things, being identified. The second scenario is to use the approach to explore a specific idea. The approach is much the same, but the aim is to ensure we start with a stakeholder perspective and use this to develop a better understanding of the opportunity and its implications.

The IT and Change Portfolio[T]: clarifying strategic alignment

An important starting point for realizing value from investments in IT is the **IT and Change Portfolio**. This describes the investments in applications and services (those already in place, those planned and future possible applications), not in terms of technology but in terms of their role and contribution to business performance (Figure 3.4). The portfolio enables senior business and IT managers to work together to get a clearer focus on doing the right things: setting priorities and ensuring strategic alignment of investments in IT-enabled change. The portfolio is based on a paper by McFarlan (Harvard Business Review, 1981) and work by Ward & Peppard (see their book Strategic Planning for Information Systems, 2002).

IT & Change Portfolio

	Strategic	Exploratory
Transformational change / doing new things	*critical to* achieving strategic objectives	*may be important* in achieving future success
Improving the current business	*critical to existing* business operations	*valuable but* *not critical* to success
	Core Operations	Support

Figure 3.4: The IT and change portfolio

(Based on Ward and Daniels (2006) & McFarlan (1981))

There are four classes of contribution to business performance. *Core Operations* systems are those where the IT is so embedded and necessary that if the system failed the organization would suffer extensively, e.g. an airline booking system. In any given industry or sector, organizations will have more or less the same Core Operations portfolio.

Support systems are about efficiency improvement. Their failure does not have far-reaching consequences, e.g. training records unavailable for a week. Eventually, of course, if the records remained unavailable for a significant period there would be some impact on performance.

IT and Change Portfolio: Examples

It is dangerous to give examples as they might be turned into rules – for example, Customer Relationship Management is Strategic. There are no rules. It all depends on the strategy and strategic context of the organization.

The first ATM (cash machine) was Strategic for a while. But then it was copied by the rest of the retail banking industry and became Core

Operations. Now many banks do not own any ATMs and are just part of a consortium. So, for these banks they are Support.

When we explored the systems used by my consulting group we felt that a spreadsheet was the only Strategic application – it was used to allocate people (always a scarce resource) to projects.

The difference between Strategic and Exploratory is often about scale and confidence (certainty). The real value of an Exploratory project may be to reduce the risk of a multi-million dollar Strategic project.

Watch out: may people refer to projects as 'strategic' when they are big, perhaps 'bet the business' projects. These are often Core Operations.

Figure 3.5: Examples of investments related to the IT and Change portfolio

Strategic and *Exploratory* are quite different – they both concern themselves with the future. Strategic systems are not just very big systems – they are those that genuinely contribute to the business's plans and strategies. When these are implemented, people will work in very different ways – ways that will confer a competitive advantage, for instance. The system does not deliver the strategic benefit – that comes from the change in the way business will be done, but the system is nevertheless crucial to the business change, e.g. an integrated international supply chain systems needed for truly global operation.

Exploratory investments are the Research & Development of IT activity – prototypes and pilots - of ideas that may confer large benefits. These projects are the basis for innovation. The uncertainty means that large sums of money should *not* be laid out until some preliminary business experimentation has taken place to explore if the benefits really exist and how they can be realized.

In a business value sense the portfolio charts the benefit life cycle of an IS investment: a promising idea is tested for proof of benefits as an Exploratory activity, if it is worthwhile it is implemented and confers Strategic advantage. Because it is good, it is copied by the industry and thus is classed as Core Operations. In time, as better IT offerings emerge; the application may migrate to Support.

The portfolio can be used to help review current IT systems and services; to manage current projects; and to explore priorities for future investments in IT. It provides a very powerful basis for bringing together senior business and IT stakeholders to make informed decisions based on a common, business oriented language.

Our challenge is to decide whether to proceed with more detailed investigation of an idea so we can move forward with a successful investment. The IT and Change portfolio allows key stakeholders to discuss and agree the potential strategic contribution of a specific idea. This might cause some debate, particularly at this early stage, but it is helpful to take an initial view on where an investment sits in the portfolio. It might make sense to investigate further an idea in any area of the portfolio, but the reasons would be different. For example, in Support – as the definition is 'valuable but not critical', we should avoid making changes unless there is a clear financial payback. In Strategic and Exploratory innovation will be a key driver and alignment with strategic objectives, and creation of new sources of value are likely to be important.

Ready to move forward?

Using Stakeholder Expectations and the IT and Change portfolio will provide new insights into an idea and whether to proceed with further investigation. We have not focused on cost or a return on investment analysis in any detail at this stage – that comes later.

The key at this stage is that the tools are simple to use. They provide a way for a small group of people to explore an idea and learn about the possibilities by working together. Although there will be an output on paper from the process, the key result is a shared understanding of the opportunity and hopefully a growing basis for working together on this or future opportunities.

The output from the work should include a 'one pager' summarizing the opportunity and making a recommendation (Figure 3.6). It usually makes sense to write up the stakeholder analysis, particularly if this is done in 'real-time' as part of the workshop. Recommendations can include: proceed with more detailed investigation straight away; proceed but at some agreed future date (for example after the year end); worth investigating at some point; or no further action.

Work on the idea may continue or it may now be clear that it is part of a bigger strategic initiative. Moving ahead requires commitment of valuable resources so a key element of the decision to proceed has to be to think about who are the right people to involve in the next stage, what level of effort is required, and if they have the time available.

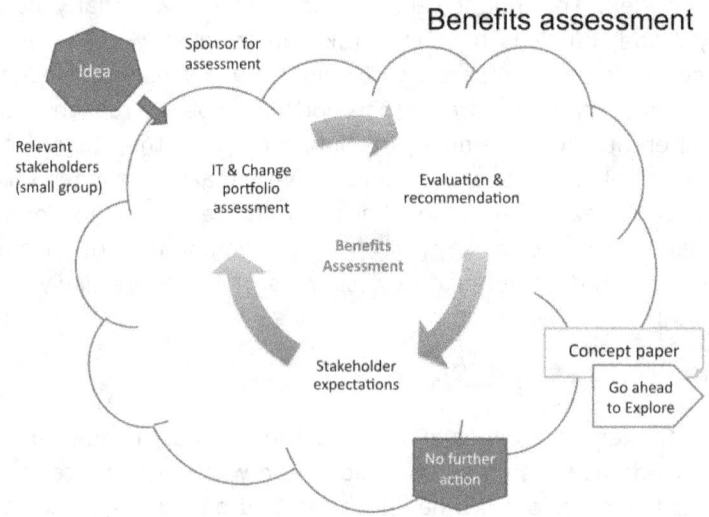

Concept Paper
A very short (1 page) summary of the opportunity.
- Why is it worth doing? (strategic contribution and portfolio contribution)
- What are the benefits? (for customers, other stakeholders and the organization as a whole)
- Who are the key players? (to move forward from here)
- How does it leverage existing resources and capabilities?
- What are the main areas of uncertainty and risk?

Figure 3.6: Outline of the Benefits Assessment and Concept Paper

Making it happen

Two big questions remain: who should be involved at this stage and who makes the decision about going ahead? To a certain extent, these are unanswerable in general – it depends on the organization and the idea. For example, at this stage it might seem that the impact is within a particular department, but this might change as a greater understanding develops. In practical terms, the investigation should involve representatives of those who might be planning and delivering the investment (IT function?) as well as potential sponsors and business areas affected. At this stage, there is no need to be comprehensive, work with customers and other directly affected stakeholders might come later.

The need for broader engagement in the decision will depend on the seniority of the sponsor engaged to date and the scale of the opportunity. It usually makes sense to share the decision making process with one or more groups that can provide a broader perspective, for example, of a product roadmap or IT strategy and architecture. There is an important balance to strike here – particularly as we are focusing on enabling innovation. Shared decision-making can be a good thing and, approached in the right way, valuable insight and additional resources can be gathered in the process. There is also a major risk that all innovation is killed by over-cautious committee based decision-making. Engage is about focusing the entrepreneurial effort and must not inadvertently kill it. It needs to be a short, value-adding process.

In summary

Engage brings momentum to a project from the beginning. It enables resources to be focused on high value opportunities to make a rapid, initial assessment of the value of further action.

***

4   Refining the plan: Explore

Key topics covered in this chapter:

o   *The focus on success through people underpins this stage as it does the rest of the project.*

o   *Driver Analysis builds on the work done earlier in the project to explore the potential strategic alignment and contribution.*

o   *Work is carried out to define the potential benefits in more detail and understand the business changes required to deliver them.*

o   *A stakeholder analysis provides a basis for planning communications, engagement and change activities in more detail.*

o   *A number of perspectives on design are taken to complement the benefits focus. The user-centred design activities are an important enabler of further innovation at this stage of the project.*

o   *The benefits realization plan is developed to pull together the work to date. It demonstrates what the benefits are and how they will be realized providing the basis for a further go / no-go decision.*

The goal: developing the Benefits Realization Plan

As we enter the Explore stage, we are going to be working on an opportunity, which has been the subject of preliminary work during Engage. The goal is to develop a Benefits Realization Plan and an initial Solution Concept prior to a critical decision point on further investment.

There are a number of activities at this stage, each supported by key elements of the toolkit. Initially we will take a step-by step approach to explain how the tools can be used in the development of the benefits realization plan. Later in the chapter, we will explore how the approach might vary in different scenarios. One key issue to consider is whether there is a decision, in principle, that a project will go ahead and that this work is about shaping the project and starting to build a team so that momentum is gained to deliver the benefits. Alternatively, a more tentative approach can be adopted with the Benefits Realization Plan as the basis for a stronger go / no-go decision, building the team and the momentum of the project can be deferred until the next stage (Evolve).

Benefits Management is "the process of organizing and managing such that the potential benefits arising from the use of IT are actually realized." Its contribution is that it provides concepts and techniques to enable the project team to focus on managing the project to ensure the benefits are realized. Other approaches focus solely on evaluating the benefits. Benefits Management is designed to bring them about. In this chapter, as elsewhere, we are drawing on these ideas. **See the book Benefits Management for more information (Ward & Daniel (2006) published by Wiley)**.

In this chapter we consider key activities involved in the Explore stage: driver analysis which builds directly on the work done during Engage. These include: the benefits and change assessment; stakeholder analysis; exploring perspectives on design; and, finally, developing a benefits realization plan (Figure 4.1).

Key activities during Explore

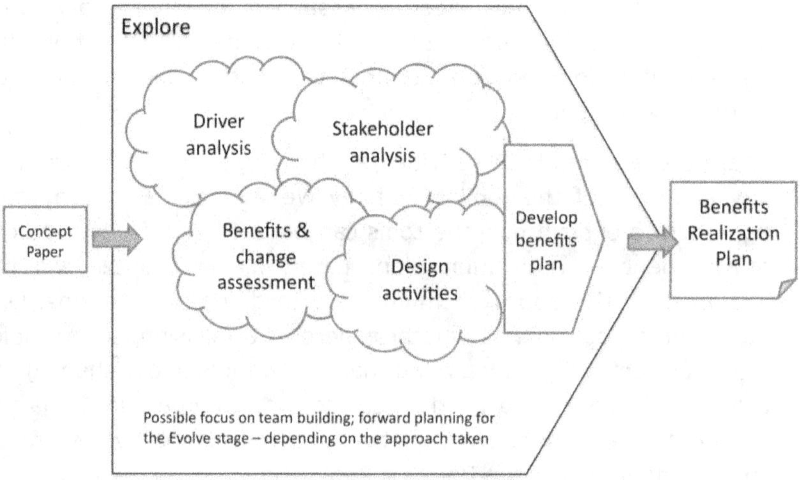

Figure 4.1: Key activities during the explore stage.

Start with the end in mind – the Benefits Realization Plan[T]

The benefits realization plan identifies (Figure 4.2):

- Why the project is required and what the high level goals are.
- What the benefits are, and for each benefit...
- How they will be measured and what the targets are.
- When they are due to arise.
- Which stakeholders they relate to.
- Who is responsible for delivery.
- What business changes are required to realize them (and who is responsible for these changes).
- What enablers are required in support of the business changes, including IT functionality.

The questions themselves can be used as a checklist when preparing and reviewing a business case. This works for new practitioners of a benefits-driven approach who are not yet familiar with the specific techniques, and for experts it is a way to summarize the key issues.

Developing the benefits realisation plan: key questions

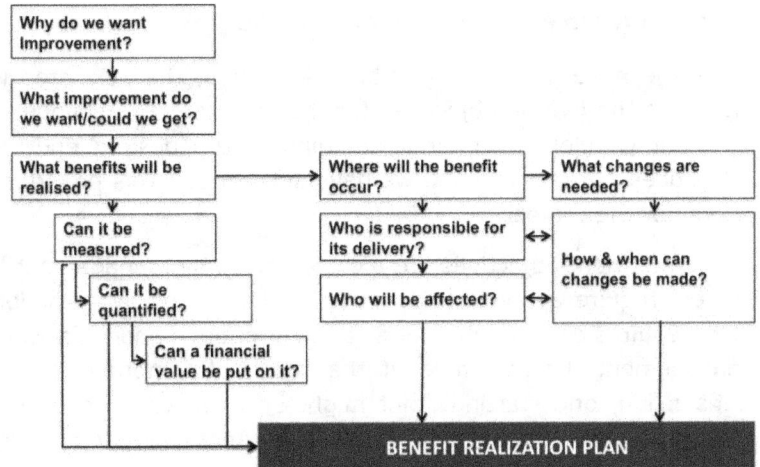

Based on Benefits Management (2006) Ward and Daniel

Figure 4.2: Outline of benefits planning - key questions

The outcome of benefits planning will be a benefits delivery or benefits realization plan setting out *what* the benefits are and *how* they are going to be realized. Although in theory all these topics should be covered by a business case, it is likely that in practice the focus is on *what* the benefits will be, rather than *how* they are realized. In addition, in many cases the approval of the business case is just another hurdle to be tackled and for many reasons the project then becomes an IT-driven technology implementation. The aim of the benefits realization plan is that it continues to have a central role in the management of the project.

It is worth exploring in more detail what we mean by these questions.

Why do we want improvement?

The crucial starting point is to get a clear understanding of why there is a need to do anything. Change is risky so we need to have a good reason for starting. This requires a good understanding of the problem or opportunity and a decision by (senior) management that action is required. We refer to the reasons change is required as the 'business drivers' or drivers.

What improvement do we want / could we get?

Once the need for action has been identified, the next step is to agree on the overall objectives for the investment in change. This is about developing an understanding of the desired end-state: what does it look like when we have succeeded? This provides the vision for the project.

The investment objectives are a choice made by management. The drivers require action, but in most circumstances, what action to take requires consideration of a range of options and a decision by management. For example, if the goal is to improve customer satisfaction, one starting point might be to invest in a customer relationship management (CRM) system. Another option would be to change employee recruitment practices. Yet another response would be to re-assess product and service design.

Many projects fail at this point because the *why* and the *what* are not clear or at least they have been defined in technical terms.

If the problem is particularly complex and messy, as they often are, it can be helpful to use Soft Systems techniques as a way of getting a better understanding of what the problem is and what would be an improvement (see for example: Learning for Action by Peter Checkland and John Poulter (2006) John Wiley & Sons).

What benefits will be realized?

Having established the objectives, the next step is to clarify the benefits for relevant groups of stakeholders. Essentially, the question to consider is: "what benefits would need to be realized to enable us to say that the objectives have been achieved?" This provides more detail to build on the initial statements of the objectives.

Where will the benefits occur?

Where will the benefits occur? Often, a change will have impacts in many areas of the organization. Which departments / business units / business processes are affected and where will any benefits show up in departmental performance metrics or in business process performance measures?

At this stage it is also important to consider the benefits and the extent to which they can be measured or quantified, and if a financial benefit can be agreed.

What changes are needed?

What changes are needed to bring about the benefits? This question requires a response in some detail to make clear what areas of the business need to change and how. For example changes may include training and education; structures; roles; locations; performance measures; reward and recognition; processes; working practices; behavior; leadership. The approach to change will vary to reflect the context and which aspects of the business are being changed.

Who is responsible for delivery?

Who is responsible for delivery of the benefits (and the changes required to bring them about)? Depending on the responses to the previous question this is likely to be senior managers across the business who are responsible for the department and process performance measures affected. This provides a fresh insight into the changes required and the potential difficulty of the project.

Who will be affected?

As a result of the previous analysis it now starts to become clear which stakeholders are affected and in what way. Who will benefit? Where will dis-benefits occur? What are the implications for the change programme and benefits realization?

How and when can changes be made?

As a result of the previous questions it should now be possible to consider how / if the necessary changes can be made and develop the Benefits Realization Plan.

These questions provide another starting point for putting benefits planning into action. They provide the basis for a quick review of an investment proposal or an initial, rapid planning exercise.

Focus on people: enabling innovation

The detailed tools and techniques are simply a means to an end – which is enabling a group of people to work together effectively to explore a valuable opportunity; develop a vision and concept for the solution and develop a benefits realization plan.

The key success factor is getting the right people working together as effectively as possible. This is far from trivial and it will often be particularly challenging to bring together a group representing different areas of the organization, with different backgrounds and skills, with different objectives and perspectives on priorities, to work together to innovate in products, services and ways of working. The tools presented here can and do enable this process, but using the tools must not become an end in itself. The skills of the facilitator and the team as a whole are critical.

It is particularly important to approach this stage of the project as a creative activity. The traditional model is often to carry out a series of interviews capturing details of possible benefits and requirements and then to compile a consolidated list. Our focus is on a series of *workshop* activities, which allow people to work and think together, and which provide an opportunity for a more in-depth exploration of possible improvements. The benefits realization plan is only one outcome, more important is to start to build a team of people with a shared vision for the potential benefits and a commitment to bringing them about. Techniques such as brainstorming and the ability to design and facilitate effective workshops, which stimulate ideas and energy, are essential.

Driver Analysis[T]

Driver Analysis is a way to investigate 'why do we want the improvement?' and 'what are the overall objectives of the investment?' It clarifies the potential contribution of the project to the organizational strategy (strategic alignment) and as a result, helps set the priority for the project. Driver analysis builds on the work already done on Stakeholder Expectations, typically bringing in a strategic, top-down perspective to complement the 'bottom-up' stakeholder focus.

Understanding the drivers reveals the strength of ownership for the project at senior levels in the business. It clarifies how the investment should link into business plans and allows IT expenditure proposals to be seen as an investment in developing the organization's capability. The rationale for analyzing the drivers is that:

- The beginning is the best place to stop bad projects (weak or insufficient rationale).

- It sets out how the investment should link into business plans both in terms of project objectives and scope.

- It reveals the strength of ownership at senior levels in the business and identifies the Sponsor(s) and their interests.

- At a high level, it determines how success will be recognized.

- It locates IT expenditure proposals as an investment in the future of the organization's capability – not merely parting with money to acquire modern technology.

A 'driver' is something that is putting pressure on the organization to change in some way. Driver analysis aims to understand the Drivers, and then decide on Investment Objectives for the project. The 'Investment Objective' is a high-level statement of the desired end state, i.e. just where the finishing-line is in the race. It doesn't cover what has to be done to get there, nor how – those choices can be delegated to stakeholder managers, project managers and other specialists who are equipped to help exploit the technology.

It worth noting that by their nature Drivers cannot be changed or made to go away – they exist independently of any kind of programme or project. The Investment Objectives represent what an organization *chooses* to do about the drivers.

Techniques for Driver Analysis

The analysis of competitive position is a key technique for driver analysis (Figure 4.3 and 4.4). The technique works at two levels. Firstly, it can be used to consider the overall competitive positioning of the organization. Which of the three dimensions is the primary focus of the organizational strategy: customer intimacy, operational excellence and product leadership?

The logic is that successful organizations will focus – not try to be best at everything. If this can be agreed, it provides valuable context and focus for the more detailed analysis and planning activities.

Organization	Strategic focus
Apple	Product innovation: leading edge products or services.
Amazon	Customer intimacy: unique value-adding solutions.
Ryanair	Operational excellence: focus on best value.

Figure 4.3: Strategic focus of well-known organizations

(adapted from Treacy and Weisma, 1993)

Then, at a second level, managers are asked to assess where they are in relation to their competition for each of the three dimensions. The assessment is carried out for each customer segment or business unit as appropriate. Is your organisation better or worse than the competition and by how much (from -5 (much worse) to +5 much better)? A score of '0' means you are equivalent to the competition. The positioning is relative and will change over time as, by doing nothing, the relative position will erode because of competitive activity.

Projects addressing 'Survival' are usually copying the rest of the sector or industry in order to catch up. Those on the same level of competitors are typically either 'business as usual' or incremental improvement. Those designed to take the business 'ahead' (to 'Prosperity') may have a radical change aspect to them since by definition no one else in the industry is doing things this way.

It is worth paying attention to the combinations of dimensions since ultimately they interact, e.g. good customer intimacy cannot be sustained for long if operations are below average and there is no clear product leadership.

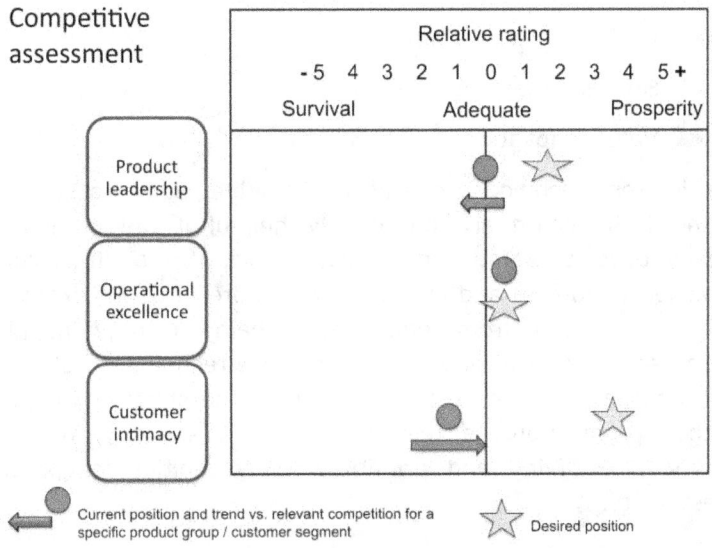

Figure 4.4: Competitive assessment
(adapted from Treacy and Weisma, 1993)

There is a need to be reasonably persistent at the driver analysis stage since this is the point where it is best to rescope projects or kill ones that should never start in the first place. The competitive assessment technique has proved very successful in helping to structure the discussions around drivers and what needs to be done about them. It attempts to set the drivers into the context of the organization's environment, especially its market place. The technique also has the virtue that it is easily understood and quickly applied.

Other tools and techniques that can help identify drivers and objectives include:

- 5-forces

- Value chain analysis

- Balanced scorecard

- Critical success factors

- Strategy mapping

- Value innovation.

The different techniques can all be valuable. Some, such as the Balanced Scorecard are particularly helpful if the organization already uses it. Some can be used quickly in a discussion or workshop (5-forces) and others need a more in-depth exercise to get the real value from them (value chain, strategy mapping). When used as part of driver analysis these techniques help clarify how a potential investment contributes to the strategic objectives of the organization. In the context of IT strategy, the focus becomes identifying and prioritizing opportunities for potential investments.

The Contribution of Driver Analysis

The output from driver analysis is a clear understanding of the Business Drivers for the project / programme and agreed Investment Objectives. These provide the basis for further work. Essentially the aim is to be able to show how the goals of the project contribute to the strategic objectives of the organization.

The IT and Change Portfolio plays an important role in driver analysis as well as in the rest of the project. The portfolio provides a powerful shorthand for exploring and describing the contribution of the proposed investment to the strategy of the organization. The fit of the investment(s) with the portfolio was first considered during Engage. At this stage it is important to re-visit the portfolio and re-assess where the planned investment(s) are.

If a project appears to be spread across several elements of the Portfolio it is possible it should be treated as a programme and split into components that each relate to one area of the portfolio. As the portfolio implies different projects need to be managed in different ways, it can be difficult to manage a project in the appropriate way if it does not fit in any one category.

It is important to develop shared use of key terms to avoid misunderstandings and to enable a clear focus on a number of important issues such as ownership for project goals vs. ongoing performance of an operational service (Figure 4.5).

Key Terminology

Project: an initiative with specific goals, resources and timescales.

Programme: a broader strategic initiative, typically including a number of projects.

Service (or business process): the operational, business as usual activity, which is the target of the changes, introduced by the project or programme.

***

All too often, we see great confusion because these concepts are not used. A project merges into an ongoing programme of change; neither of which has accountabilities that are clearly distinguished from those for management of the ongoing service.

Figure 4.5: Key terminology – project, programme and service

Benefits and Change Analysis[T]

Having identified the drivers and investment objectives, the next stage is to identify the benefits that need to be delivered. A workshop approach is used to create a 'benefit dependency network' (BDN – Figure 4.6) that relates the business drivers with the project deliverables, including the IT solution. This network establishes a clear understanding of the overall business change plan and the contribution of technology.

The starting point for the benefits dependency network is the set of drivers and investment objectives already defined. The next stage is to consider what benefits would be realized if the investment objectives are achieved. The aim is to identify benefits relevant to specific stakeholders. One way to do this is to have a large wall, a very large whiteboard or a number of sheets of flipchart paper available. Each benefit is then written on a 'post-it' note that can be stuck onto the network. The 'enabling changes' and 'business changes' respectively define the one-off and ongoing changes in the business that are necessary to realize the benefits. Once the benefits have been identified, the business changes and then enabling changes are identified in a similar interactive process and positioned on the network using 'post-its'. The logic to consider each benefit in turn and ask 'what needs to be done differently for this benefit to be achieved?' It can be a messy process, but the use of 'post-its' enables changes to be made.

A key contribution of the technique is the discussion that it generates in the workshop. This plays a key role in building a shared vision for the project. The workshop is often most effective if the business sponsor for the project is fully involved. The physical environment is also important – it is important that there is room for people move around, and to stand by the evolving network.

Although the network is built from right to left, once it has been developed, it can be read from left to right. It represents the cause and effect logic that underpins the project: if we implement the specified IT, make one-off enabling changes to the business and start to work in new ways (the business changes) the required benefits will be achieved. As a result, we will have achieved the desired investment objectives, which have been defined in response to the drivers for change.

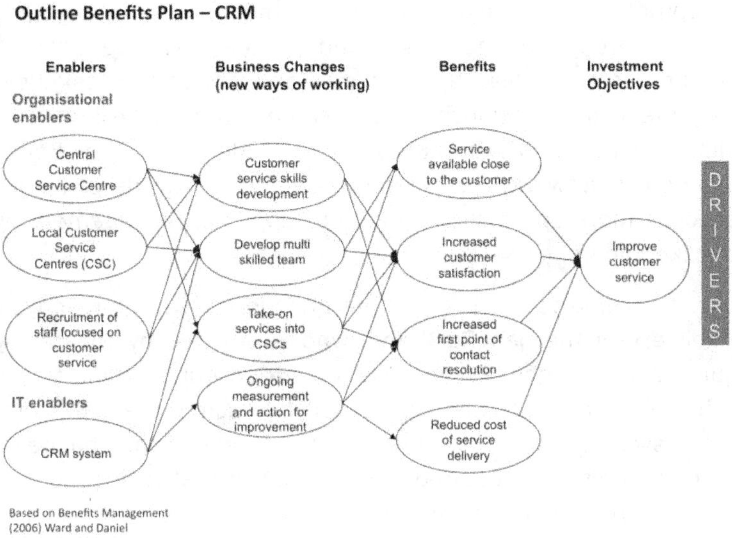

Outline Benefits Plan – CRM

Figure 4.6: The Benefits Dependency Network
(a simplified example based on a customer service / CRM programme)

The BDN comes directly from the work of John Ward on Benefits Management – see Further Reading.

The network forms the basis for the two elements of the benefits delivery plan, i.e. 'what are the benefits?' and 'how are they going to be delivered?' Subsequent practices validate and refine the results from the development of the network.

Alternative Techniques

The Benefits Roadmap (see Information Paradox by John Thorp published by Wiley) is a technique that can be used at this stage instead of the Benefits Dependency Network.

Stakeholder Analysis[T] and relationship development

There are many aspects to stakeholder analysis and relationship development. The focus on engagement with stakeholders continues throughout the project and the team will use a range of different perspectives to explore and manage stakeholder engagement and relationships. The stakeholder analysis approach outlined here is a structured tool building on the Benefits Dependency Network; we typically use this alongside other tools that focus more specifically on how to approach *engagement* with the stakeholders.

Stakeholder analysis addresses the questions: 'who is responsible for delivery of the benefits?' and 'who is affected by the changes required?' A 'stakeholder analysis' is carried out to think through the benefits and 'dis-benefits' related to each stakeholder group and to assess the existing level of commitment to the change, the level of commitment required, and the action that is needed to get to the required level of commitment

A typical situation is that one group receives the benefits and another group is supposed to work differently so that the benefits are delivered. Often the benefits are not realized because of the mis-match of the lack of appropriate actions to manage the changes required.

Identification of all the stakeholders, and analysis of their perspectives and attitudes to the changes implied by the project, is essential since no benefits will emerge if their involvement is not correctly managed. The following needs to be done:

- All stakeholders have to be identified.

- Their perceptions on Benefits, Dis-benefits, and Resistance, if any, need to be understood.

- Any changes that are needed by them must be made explicit.

- Their commitment to the project should be established together with an appreciation of whether it needs to be changed or embraced in some other way.

One approach, developed by Benjamin and Levinson, which has shown itself to be effective, is the structured use of the form in Figures 4.6 and 4.7.

Page 66

Each group of stakeholders is identified and their perceived benefits (or dis-benefits) are established. Any changes that the group itself must undertake for the benefits to appear are documented, as is their perceived resistance to those changes. This information is largely available from the Benefits Dependency Network.

Stakeholder analysis (I):
linking the benefits and the changes

Stakeholder	Changes needed	Perceived benefits (& dis-benefits)	Perceived benefits

after Benjamin & Levinson (1993)

Figure 4.6: Stakeholder analysis
(based on Benjamin and Levinson, 1993)

An assessment of the current capability of the stakeholders to adapt to the change is made (Figure 4.7). The next five columns are an aid to assessing the stakeholders' commitment and, hence, the amount of managing that has to be done to get the right degree of involvement. For each group, a 'C' (= current commitment) is marked in the appropriate column (e.g. 'anti') then an 'R' (= required commitment) is marked in the column where the stakeholder 'needs to be'. Clearly, the further apart the C and R are the greater the amount of change intervention is needed. The final column is then used to record any actions required. These actions are new Changes and Enabling Changes in the benefits network.

Stakeholder analysis (II):
linking the benefits and the changes

Stakeholder	Commitment				Recommended Actions
	Anti	Let it happen	Help it happen	Make it happen	

after Benjamin & Levinson (1993)

**Figure 4.7: Stakeholder analysis
(based on Benjamin and Levinson, 1993)**

4.6 and 4.7 are normally combined into one form

Experience shows that any stakeholder who is one column to the left of where they 'should be' can usually be influenced by their manager to make the transition (e.g. from *Anti* to *None* or *Allow to Help*). Where the change in commitment is two or more columns, there is an explicit change management task to be addressed. It must be addressed, or otherwise the new way of working, and hence the benefits, will not happen. Where the transition needed is three or more columns, the stakeholder's position is likely to be more of a "hearts and minds" issue. Very firm instruction will not work since the recipient is responding less from the head and more from how he/she feels about the changes; they may feel very threatened and confused, so rational debate cannot be the first step.

It also follows that any 'two or more column shifts' should be entered in the Dependency Network as enabling changes. Most workshops in creating Benefit Dependency Networks find it relatively easy to identify 'hard' enabling changes, such as "Rewrite Standards Manual to meet ISO9000" or "Design New Procedure". However, the 'softer' people-oriented issues either get missed or dismissed sometimes under the easy catch-all of "Culture and Politics" which technical personnel can regard as outside their domain of interest.

It is helpful to look at the overall set of stakeholders and to consider the various inter-relationships and priorities (Figure 4.8). It is usually wise to focus on those stakeholders who will experience the most changes. However, those who will get a lot of benefit but experience little change need managing as well since they can become impatient with other stakeholders and try to force unreasonable rates of change progress, causing adverse reaction and sometimes disruption.

New benefits should not appear at this point. If discussion shows there may be more, then the Benefits Network activity needs revisiting. Appearance of more benefits could indicate that the attendees at the initial workshops were not representative enough.

Remember it is Perceived Benefits and Perceived Dis-benefits that matter here, since ultimately Stakeholder reaction always boils down to one question: "What's in it for me?" - a question that should always be answered even if the answer is unpopular.

Stakeholders – interest/influence model

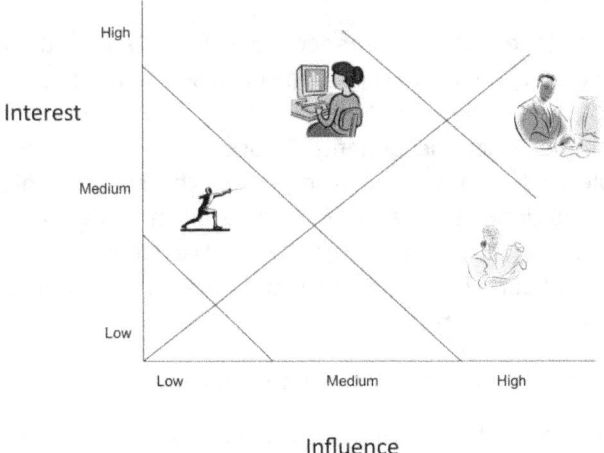

Figure 4.8: Stakeholder analysis - the bigger picture

Success in stakeholder analysis can be judged by the following:

- All stakeholders are identified, informed and involved to an appropriate degree.

- All perceptions and commitments are documented and agreed as representing the current situation.

- Managers agree how the improvements will be tackled.

- Dis-benefits are properly discussed, documented and a management response is given, or a date when the response will be forthcoming.

- There is sufficient clarity and agreement of the changes needed to form the entries in the Benefits Plan for explanation and discussion with the sponsor.

- Change responsibilities are documented as part of the project documentation.

Design perspective

It is important to take a design perspective at this stage and start to explore aspects of the solution concept or design. The emphasis on this perspective will vary from project to project. This perspective complements the benefits focused work by exploring what is possible and starting to consider what the solution might look like. In a traditional approach, this would often follow later or be approached as procurement of a solution. We view this as an important element of the innovation process, which will add considerable value to the project.

From requirements gathering to user-centered design

A classic starting point for an IT project is to ask the users what their requirements are for a new system. Of course, some organizations bypass this step by letting senior management decide. In any case, there are a number of serious flaws.

What if the senior management view of the drivers for change and the high level objectives has not (yet) been communicated effectively to other stakeholders? If communication has taken place, what if the users and other stakeholders have different ideas and priorities? Perhaps senior management have a vision based on dramatically improving customer service, but the front line staff are under so much pressure they can only envisage incremental changes to do away with some of the most pressing problems and causes of inefficiency? The requirements provided by the end users are likely to be only loosely related to the vision defined by management.

In a scenario involving innovation, whether involving new technology or not, all stakeholders are likely to have trouble envisaging what is possible. Sessions to 'gather requirements' or document the 'as is' situation of the business process are likely to be of only limited value.

A further mindset shift is required. This time from requirements gathering to innovation through user-centered design. The approach required is to engage a multi-disciplinary team in a process of exploration and innovation, which builds from the initial understanding of the opportunity to a vision and initial (conceptual) design. A number of different practices can contribute insights to the design process.

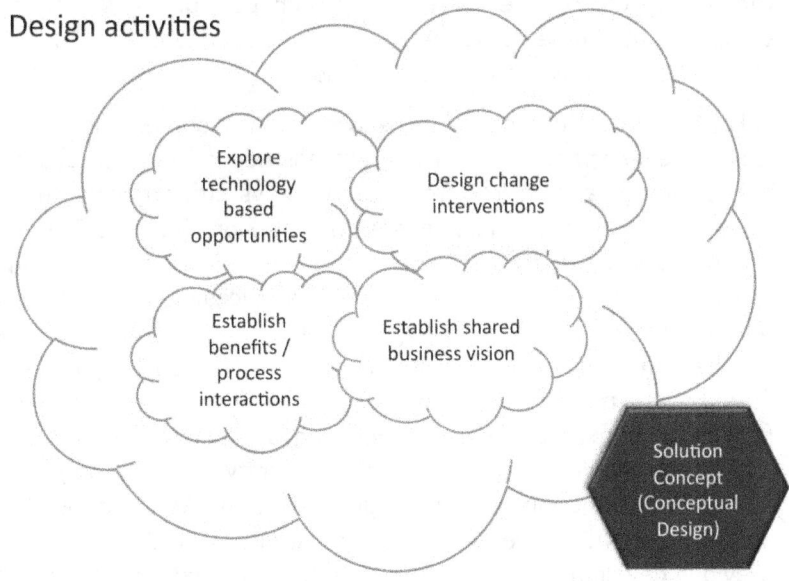

Figure 4.9: Design activities explored in this chapter

Exploring the technology based opportunities

The design process should involve consideration of the problems / opportunities from a user perspective and the opportunities provided by the technology. An understanding of the technology provides insight into what is possible and which options are easy to accomplish. The focus on the opportunities enabled by the technology helps to break out of making incremental improvements to the current situation and can provide an opportunity for business innovation.

Important implications of this practice are:

- The need for good knowledge of the technology within the team.

- An approach to the project lifecycle that allows learning.

In early IT developments, a waterfall (sequential) development process worked well. The project effectively started with a 'clean sheet of paper' and the initial focus of activity was getting a detailed understanding of user requirements. All functionality required to deliver the solution was then part of the design and development. Some companies even developed operating system software and hardware following this logic.

Following this approach today is a serious mistake. There is no 'clean sheet of paper'. The design process needs to take account of the services available from the operating system, other purchased software (database, email, messaging, etc) or available from the 'cloud' from a rapidly increasing range of pay-as-you-go service providers. There will be very extensive services, such as security, backup, transactional integrity, audit trails, error handling, that can be simply incorporated into a solution. In addition, in many cases, there may be significant application functionality that can be used. For example, when developing an ecommerce site most organizations will incorporate purchased software providing much of the core functionality (catalogue, sales basket and pipeline, sales analysis). There will also be services to draw on from previous development projects within the organization. As a result, a successful project needs people with good knowledge of the technologies being used and the existing systems of the organization.

With new products / technologies the full potential may not be clear even to the creators and suppliers. It is normal to find that new uses and the best ways to use the technology gradually emerge through experience and learning in the real world. The incremental approach to phased delivery of benefits is an important enabler of learning.

Opportunity-based design applies to all projects. The need for this focus on opportunities is particularly strong when the project is implementation of a software package (ERP, CRM, etc). In this case, it is essential to start from gaining an understanding of what the software can do and exploring which of the available options provides the best solution. One recent case study we carried out revealed serious issues in this area. A package solution had been selected at a higher level in the organization and had been effectively imposed at a local level. The local implementation project did not compensate for the lack of requirements and selection process and the project became focused on technology implementation because there had not been a need to focus on the business problem and user needs.

In summary, following a 'clean sheet of paper' approach and driving the design just from user requirements can result in missed opportunities for new ways of working, and solutions that are not a good fit with the technology, are higher risk, and take longer to deliver.

Establish Benefits and Business Process Interaction[T]

A second practice to consider as part of the design perspective is to consider benefits and process interactions. The business area involved is considered as a process. A process has inputs, activities and outputs. Improvements can be made in terms of cost, speed and quality. Taking these aspects of a process produces a 3 by 3 matrix as shown in Figure 4.8.

The practice can be used as a starting point to get an understanding of a scenario. In addition, if a benefits dependency network has already been developed, the 3 by 3 process perspective can be used to explore the completeness of the benefits identified. The benefits identified are mapped onto the 3 by 3 matrix. This typically identifies gaps in the analysis carried out when the BDN is prepared and is a starting point for the identification of further possible benefits that fill in the gaps.

Identifying opportunities for improvement: taking a process perspective

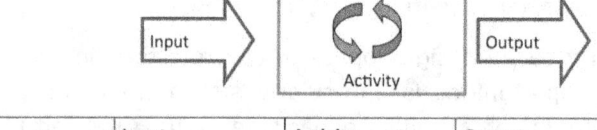

	Input	Activity	Output
Cost	?	Reduced cost of service delivery	Ongoing measurement to drive further improvements
Speed	Customer able to gain access to service close to home	First point of contact resolution	?
Quality	?	First point of contact resolution	Increased customer satisfaction

Figure 4.8: A business process perspective on benefits
(a simplified example)

It is also possible to carry out more extensive work from a business process perspective; for example, looking at the design of target business processes. The business process perspective also has limitations. Be particularly careful in professional and knowledge work situations not to try and define a process in too much detail.

Establish a shared business vision

The overall direction and goals for the project (objectives) are captured in a vision statement. The statement is short, a sentence or at most a short paragraph. The vision statement provides clarity of purpose and a motivational target for the project team and project stakeholders. As details of requirements, solution design and project plan change, the vision statement should provide a solid foundation to which the team can return. The vision statement should have a business focus, and everyone involved in the project should share an understanding of the vision.

Example

We will set up and run a medical school in Malaysia for 400 medical students per annum with a learning experience of the same quality as the home university.

One of the causes of project failure is getting lost in the detail of requirements capture and solution design. Different groups have different requirements and there can be a rapid growth of complexity as the team try to accommodate the demands of each group. This can also result in conflict as each group fights for as much of the project resource as possible to be devoted to meeting their needs.

A second cause of failure is that understanding of the drivers for the project and the overall goals can be lost as the project progresses and different groups are involved. There may be clear business objectives in the minds of senior management, but often they are not understood or fully shared by users involved in the project or the project team.

The vision statement starts to address these issues. It provides a high level view of the objectives and direction of the project. It enables flexibility as the project progresses. It should also provide a motivational goal as the project team and other stakeholders make a commitment to realizing the vision.

Developing a short vision statement is difficult. It takes time to get the words just right. For the vision to be 'shared' there needs to be broad involvement in its development – it would typically form part of initial work on the project. At this stage, it is most effective to use a series of workshops to bring together senior management, users and key project team members.

How to make the changes happen: designing the approach to change

The benefits perspective implies that benefits are realized as a result of changes in the organization. The scale and scope of changes will vary from project to project. This practice starts to establish a framework of the different types of organizational change to help ensure that benefits planning addresses all the issues that are relevant in a particular situation.

The organization is extremely complex. It exists in a rapidly changing environment and its strategy and performance depend on the interaction of a wide range of stakeholders with different objectives and contributions. No one perspective can adequately describe the organization and in many cases it is likely that there will be unexpected results from change initiatives (both good and bad). It is important to consider the interaction of the investment with the organization as broadly as possible to consider both the potential risks and the range of interventions required to succeed in realizing the benefits.

A key starting point for this book is the resource-based perspective, which considers an organization as inter-related resources, competences and capabilities (4.9). We view this as a very powerful perspective for both developing and implementing strategy. It seems a good fit with the real world. Unfortunately, one of the drawbacks of the approach to date is that it can be hard to operationalise and there is no simple way of identifying, classifying or designing competences and capabilities.

Resources, Competences and Capabilities: an example

Capability: The organization-wide capability to consistently realize value from investments in IT-enabled change and transformation.

Competences: The four competences of benefits planning, benefits delivery; benefits exploitation and benefits review which are brought to life through the e4+1 framework and the benefits toolkit.

Resources: The skills and energy of individuals; the 'toolkit' of effective working practices; enabling organizational structures, processes and environment.

Figure 4.9: Resources, competences and capabilities – an example

If we view the organization as resources, competences and capabilities it should make sense to view the output from a business transformation programme (investment in IT) as new or changed resources, competences and capabilities. So, an important perspective on design is the practice of designing business competences.

Business competence-based design works at two broad levels. Firstly, it helps consider the outcome of the investment as new and improved resources, competences and capabilities. Secondly, it helps define these elements in more detail and explore the implications for the changes that are required. We need to use a range of perspectives to address the real-world complexity of an organization in developing a design for a new business solution including:

- Process – normally the starting point. The process can be defined as 'the activities involved in delivering value to a stakeholder'.

- Practices – how people actually work. It is important to consider this perspective as well as the process perspective, particularly in the many situations where the people have considerable discretion in how they approach activities.

- Roles and skills – the jobs and skill requirements for individuals.

- Structures – the formal organizational structure (geographical, product based, process based, span of control, etc).

- Information (and knowledge) – required to do the job and to manage and improve the process.

- Management framework – the role of management and how they influence and control.

- Performance measures – to monitor the process and to motivate individuals and teams.

- Culture – a very broad perspective on 'how we do things around here'. Frameworks, such as the 'cultural web', provide a way to explore what we mean by culture and start to consider it in planning and managing change. (For more on the cultural web (Johnson and Scholes) try your favourite search engine for some valuable resources.)

All of these 'dimensions' of an organization can be affected, sometimes significantly, by changes to information systems.

The relevance of the different perspectives will vary from project to project. A range of techniques can be applied to help address these different perspectives. The design addresses the overall business solution and not just the IT solution. The system requirements are considered in the context of each of these dimensions. A deeper understanding of the business goals also provides a good starting point for considering how to approach the different aspects of change. For example, changes to process and structures might be relatively straightforward, but working practices and behaviors may be much harder to change.

Design – summary

We have explored a design perspective and considered aspects of the business and IT solution that will contribute to benefits realization. There is much more work to do and much that is beyond the scope of this book; for example, user-centered practices for design of the system. Our aim is to promote innovation by using the design perspective alongside the other benefits-driven practices. It is important to recognize that this will be a messy, creative process, but that in many situations it provides a much greater chance of success than the more ordered linear requirements gathering process traditionally adopted.

The Benefits Realization Plan[T]

At this stage, it is possible to develop the benefits realization plan, which pulls together the results of the work on benefits planning. The benefits realization plan becomes a central part of the ongoing management of the project with project reviews and milestone reviews driven by an emphasis on "are we on track to deliver the benefits?" rather than just progress against budgets and timetables. The benefit plan is kept up to date, reflecting learning and changes during the life of the project.

The emphasis at this stage is on developing a 'benefit realization plan' that identifies:

- Benefits and how they relate to different stakeholders / stakeholder groups (a benefit is an advantage for a stakeholder).

- Owners for each benefit / benefit stream – there must be an owner to be included.

- Measures related to each benefit – if the benefit isn't measurable (in some way) it isn't a benefit.

- Who is going to do what differently - i.e. what business changes are required to deliver the benefits.

- How the changes will be brought about and who is responsible for them.

Identify benefits owners

Based on the stakeholder analysis and the other work on benefits planning, owners for each benefit are agreed. This is an important business role on the project. Benefits owners are an important part of the project governance framework. At this stage, the real level of commitment to the project will be put to the test.

Structure Benefits and Establish Targets & Measures[T]

The benefits are classified (see Figure 4.10) as to how explicit they are by ranking them as measurable, quantifiable and financial and according to whether the benefit allows:

- The business to do something *new.*

- Current activities to be improved (*better*).

- The elimination of certain activities (*stop*).

A quantifiable benefit is a measurable benefit where a specific target can be defined and agreed. For example, if the project involved increasing response rates from mail shots to customers as a result of better targeting this is clearly *measurable*. It may be possible to do some work, perhaps a pilot, to get further evidence so that a realistic target can be set and the benefit can be made *quantifiable*. The core difference is that, for the benefit to be quantifiable, we need to have a benefit owner who will sign up to take responsibility for the specific target. It is really about our level of knowledge and confidence in the forecast. Ideally, benefits will be *financial* and quantifiable but the approach recognizes that this is not always possible.

It is essential not just to dismiss non-financial benefits as 'intangible.' The quantifiable and measurable categories should be used to highlight the many benefits, for example related to customer satisfaction, that will not be *directly* financial, but that will have a major impact on organizational success in the longer term.

There should be a clear link with the IT and Change Portfolio. The extent to which the project is financially justified will depend on what type of project it is. The financial element of the plan can be presented using whatever techniques are in use within the organization (IRR, NPV, Payback Period, etc).

Developing the business case

	STOP doing things	**Do things BETTER**	**Do NEW things**
Financial	Reduced costs in back office functions	Reduced cost of service delivery	
Quantifiable		Increased first point of contact resolution	Service available close to the customer
Measurable		Improved customer satisfaction	

after Benefits Management (2006) Ward and Daniel

Figure 4.10: Structuring benefits
(a simplified example)

Effective measurement

Benefits Management emphasizes the importance of *ownership* of benefits and of appropriate *measurement* of benefits. Measures are important for two reasons:

- Effective measurement provides information on the outcome of the investment providing accountability and enabling learning.

- Measurement causes changes in behavior (what gets measured gets done) and as a result, measures are a major *driver of change* and can determine *if* the benefits arise (i.e. they don't just provide information on the benefits - the measures help bring about).

Setting the right measures that are cost effective and encourage behavior that results in the desired benefits is difficult. Unexpected effects can easily arise.

It is also important to avoid turning measurement into a new area of bureaucracy. There should be a balance between using the tools to think through the potential benefits and the changes required to realize them, with the pragmatic case for a few, carefully chosen measures that will put the focus on key areas and will contribute to the required changes.

Information for benefits tracking

An additional consideration is the need for information to track the realization of benefits. The collection, analysis and presentation of the required information needs to be considered as part of the solution design. Ideally this should link with planning for ongoing management of the performance of the new service / way of working / business process.

In many cases, it becomes clear at this stage that weaknesses in information currently available make it difficult or impossible to measure the current situation. So, it will be impossible to accurately compare 'before' and 'after'. This is usually an inconvenience, rather than a reason for not doing anything.

Identify and define costs

In theory, costs are the straightforward part of the business case / benefits realization plan and are likely to be handled more easily than benefits. However, this is not an entirely straightforward area and some aspects of costs are difficult to identify and relate to a project. This produces issues of accountability and adversely affects decision-making; for example, when comparing business cases which only contain some elements of the overall project costs, i.e. those most easily and directly attributable to the project.

The business case should address: one-off business and IT costs related to the project, including any new hardware and software; costs related to business changes; and ongoing impacts on business and IT costs. The IT costs may include allocation of expenditure related to IT infrastructure that makes a critical contribution to the project. Significant elements of these costs are often not included in business cases, which tend to focus on external and direct IT costs. In particular, the indirect costs of the business changes are often ignored.

Establishing fully accurate costing may not be possible or cost effective, for example, as many individuals in IT and business areas will spend only a part of their time on a project and are unlikely to complete timesheets that enable this information to be captured and recorded.

There are also wider factors; for example, a fear that if end-user costs are identified they will become additional, real incremental costs for the business. In this case, it may be better if the time spent on the required activities (training, process change, etc) is simply absorbed in departmental budgets. This is a strong argument, but there are other very important factors that must be addressed. In the absence of a budget that fairly represents all project costs there may be a number of unintended, adverse consequences:

- The organization may undertake non-beneficial projects (e.g. the hidden, indirect costs exceed the benefits).

- The organization may undertake the 'wrong' projects: for example, a project with low direct costs and high indirect costs is likely to be approved over a project, with higher direct costs regardless of the respective benefits.

Design a framework for business change governance

The overall aim of work at this stage is to be ready to proceed with the realization of benefits from the proposed investment in IT. The governance framework is likely to evolve from the stakeholder involvement and should be in place to approve the benefits realization plan and to lead the start of the next stage of the work.

The governance framework will ensure the right involvement and ownership for business change and benefits realization. The governance framework and related performance measures will have a significant impact on the focus of the project and the behavior of individuals. The role and contribution of the project sponsor is a key element of the governance framework.

Basic control processes can be largely the same across a wide range of projects (the existence of a project board, a business sponsor, risk management, lessons learned, etc). However, there is no single best design for a governance framework. The framework adopted should be adapted to meet the challenges of an individual project, and to take into account the experience of those involved.

Risk assessment

The causes of project failure are well known. Many of the factors that are going to cause a project to get into trouble can be seen at the start of the project and certainly well before they have an impact. We have two main responses:

- Firstly, we design our approach to the project to take into account both the major sources of risks and the associated critical success factors; for example, the team model addresses a range of risks (see Chapter 5). The practices outlined in this book address many of these areas.

- Secondly, we establish an effective risk management process that maintains a focus on risk throughout the life of the project.

The risk management process is straightforward. The key to success is to put the process into practice and *use it* throughout the life of the project. Virtually all projects make some attempt at risk management. However, in many cases it is not used effectively.

A crucial success factor is to take a benefits perspective to risk management:

- *Scope*: the context for the risk management process is the delivery of measurable benefits on behalf of stakeholders. Many risks and issues will not relate specifically to the delivery of a software solution.

- *Involvement*: the benefits focus implies that the risk management process must involve stakeholders in the business change not simply the IT solution. For example, user representatives on the project should be involved in risk meetings and the overall project governance framework should include owners of the business changes and benefits.

- *Prioritization*: the primary basis for assessing the potential impact of a risk should be in relation to the realization of benefits.

It is important to carry out an initial risk assessment as part of the development of the benefits realization plan. This activity will allow the team to stand back from the detail and reflect on their work to date.

Phase Benefits Delivery[T]

Phasing benefits delivery is a fundamental principle underpinning the e^{4+1} approach.

Many projects grow to have very long timescales and very large project teams. Both these factors increase the complexity of project management – exponentially. Keeping the duration of projects short (say, 4-6 months) and using small teams significantly reduces their complexity and dramatically increases their chance of success. This approach also has the benefit of reducing the exposure of the project to changes in the organization or the market during the life of the project. Additional, major, benefits are that the short project timescale means that 'time to benefit' is reduced and that there is an early opportunity to learn from the live operation of the service.

The implication is that large projects must be broken up into 'chunks' that can be delivered in 4-6 months. This is usually possible. Each small project is then seen as a 'versioned release' contributing to the overall project or programme goals. The split of a project into a number of versions can also enable different approaches to be taken to different versions, for example, based on the IT and Change portfolio. In many scenarios, where there is significant innovation and change, the only real way to learn about what the end-user or customer actually wants is to get an initial version of the service in live operation.

This approach is also called 'iterative and incremental development'. Each version or iteration must contain functionality that enables the delivery of a new or improved service and specific benefits to stakeholders. Typically, functionality in a specific area will be delivered in stages, i.e. incrementally over a number of releases. The approach applies to both bespoke developments and software package implementations. When using a package the emphasis is on phasing the business change rather than the software development.

The versioned release approach blurs the boundary between a project and a programme. The need to use a programme management approach will largely depend on the scale of activity and, in particular, if there are a number of projects / versions being delivered in parallel.

The benefits dependency network provides a basis for breaking the objectives down into a number of projects or 'versioned releases'. It is also important that the links between the IT solution and the benefits remain clear. This traceability is important to enable effective decision making on trade-offs and changes through the life of the project.

Summary – the benefits realization plan

The benefits realization plan is a vital foundation for the project. It should provide a focus for the activity of the team in later stages. It should also be treated as a *living document* and updated to reflect learning during the project.

At this stage, as in all areas of the project, considerable judgment is required. It is vital to balance two views. Firstly, every benefit has to have a measure and an owner to be included in the benefits realization plan. Secondly, benefits and related measures are vital aspects of communicating the project and there should be a focus on a small number of benefits and very well designed measures that help stakeholders understand what the project is about and help drive the desired changes. Both views are true and need to be reconciled in some way that is appropriate for the project. For example, the benefits plan might provide a comprehensive treatment of benefits, but stakeholder communication will be driven by a core set of benefits and measures and these can subsequently be updated; for example, during Expand as the focus shifts to capturing a second tier of benefits. Benefits thinking must not be allowed to grow into an innovation killing bureaucracy – it is designed to enable innovation and contribute to project success.

The process – developing the benefits plan

Organizations are complex. They are not easy to understand. The strategy may not be written down. If it is, it may not be available outside the boardroom. The actual course of action the organization is following may not match the documented strategy. Different parts of the organization may see the strategy in different ways. Individuals and groups may have their own goals that align more or less well with the goals of the organization. In situations of innovation and change, there will be different views of the goals and the challenges in realizing them.

Top management may be focused on the competition and the reaction of shareholders. Operational management and staff are more likely to be concerned about 'keeping the show on the road' with limited resources, and will be more interested in improvements to the current situation than new innovations. Into this complex situation comes the project team trying to understand the requirements for a new system and to develop a design for the solution. There are a number of crucial areas to consider.

The benefits realization plan and stakeholder analysis along with the other techniques provide a framework for business and IT to work together with a common language and a clear understanding of the objectives in business terms. You can group the output from this stage into a number of different documents. Essentially, the deliverables form a benefits realization plan, which incorporates:

- The traditional business case.
- A vision for the project.
- An initial solution concept.
- A risk assessment.
- An initial action plan and governance framework for moving ahead to the next stage of the project.

There are various approaches to activities during the Evolve stage. The table provides some examples. A key decision is when to start to gain momentum with the project, including building the team. You will need to determine the right approach for your project. Scenarios 1-5 provide some examples (Figure 4.11)

Scenario 1

Context: the opportunity appears strong but it is hard to assess the benefits and the next steps are not clear.

Approach: plan a rapid Explore phase. Hold two workshops: one to develop the benefits dependency network as a creative process, then a second to explore stakeholder issues and options for action including phasing delivery.

Result: a clearer view of the potential benefits, greater stakeholder engagement and a basis for a targeted next stage of work on an initial design and a more detailed benefits plan (essentially a second pass at the Explore phase but with a greater focus).

Scenario 2

Context: the opportunity is interesting but it is clear that significant change is required and the solution and/or benefits are unclear.

Approach: treat as an Exploratory project. Assemble a small team and allow them to work quickly to develop either a prototype or pilot solution. Balance work on design and benefits thinking. Focus on making it real to get a better understanding of possibilities.

Result: the approach allows innovation and learning from rapid creation of a prototype or pilot output.

Scenario 3

Context: the opportunity is a major strategic initiative that is clearly aligned to strategic goals and is a priority based on the annual business plan.

Approach: identify key players who will form the nucleus of the project team, including the project sponsor and project manager. Work through key activities outlined for the Explore stage as a team, focusing on team building and establishing effective ways of working that will enable momentum in later stages of the project. Use the practices as creative techniques and do not focus on a specific solution and plan too early. Work on the assumption that the project will continue to the Evolve stage but use the end of Explore milestone as a major checkpoint to establish a baseline benefits plan, conceptual design and approach.

Result: a Strategic project is underway with clear goals and a high chance of success.

Scenario 4

Context: the opportunity appears strong but work on the benefit plan reveals lack of business ownership.

Approach: further work on the project is stopped.

Result: resources are released for priority projects. Another technology-driven project that fails to deliver benefits is avoided.

It is good practice to stop projects at this stage. Just ensure that any learning is captured to feedback into the process and the selection of ideas for exploration.

Scenario 5

Context: indications are that there will be a clear financial return on the project. The changes will affect aspects of the business that are 'valuable' but not critical.

Approach: it is a potential Support project. It is likely that it will involve relatively straightforward changes to existing ways of working. A financial business case and simple benefits realization plan should be developed next.

Result: resources are not wasted until a clear case is established. Strong foundations for a Support project are put in place without 'over-engineering.'

Figure 4.11: Adapting the approach to a project

In summary

Developing the benefits realization plan is challenging. Stakeholders genuinely have different needs and perspectives, power, and politics will intervene. Key points to remember include:

- Different stakeholders may have very different perspectives on what constitutes a desirable outcome.

- In situations of major change, there may be a significant gap between senior management and end-user views of the objectives.

- A business process perspective on the organization may capture *what* is required but often will not adequately represent *how* the work is actually done.

- The complexity of real world organizations means that the unexpected effects of change related activities complicate planning and delivering change.

- To attempt to address the complexity of organizations in the real world it is important to consider desired outcomes and the challenges of making changes from a range of perspectives.

Many approaches to IT projects give little emphasis to identifying the business problem to be solved or to the challenges of identifying the 'requirements'. Both these areas are major challenges and there is a tendency to rush into software / solution delivery without adequate problem or requirements definition. The work on developing the benefits realization plan helps make the goals of the project much clearer and ensures they are defined in business benefits terms.

***

5 Making it happen: Evolve

Key topics covered in this chapter:

- *Evolve represents the core of the project where plans and ideas turn into action.*

- *A primary focus is building the team, including the core project team and the wider group of engaged stakeholders.*

- *Delivering the planned changes requires constant energy and attention, often with a lot of focus and ownership at each local level affected by the project.*

- *Many traditional project planning and control practices remain relevant but are adopted with a different mindset.*

- *The approach enables learning and flexibility as the project continues in order to facilitate business innovation.*

Building Momentum

The emphasis in the project stages so far has been on planning. Planning is crucial. The seeds of success or failure are sown at the beginning of a project. So far, we have established a clear benefits realization plan setting out the intended benefits for stakeholders and how we are going to realize them. We have also established at least a conceptual design as a basis for further work on the business and IT solution.

Moving onto **Evolve**, the focus is now on building an effective, multi-disciplinary project team and gaining momentum to deliver the intended benefits. In many organizations, the 'project' starts at this stage after approval of a business case. Other key areas to focus on at this stage include:

- Designing the business and IT solution that will enable benefits to be realized.

- Managing change, including continued effective engagement with stakeholders.

- Maintaining control of the project.

- Enabling learning and flexibility.

In the final section, we summarize by setting out a number of critical success factors for Evolve.

Establishing the context: projects and agile approaches

Formal definitions provide a starting point for understanding "what is a project?"

> *'A unique set of activities, with definite starting and finishing points, undertaken by an individual or organization to meet specific objectives within defined schedule, cost and performance parameters'*
>
> BS6079, Association of Project Managers (APM) Body of Knowledge

It is helpful to expand on the formal definitions of a project by considering a number of general characteristics of projects.

Projects:

- Are carried out to create specific *results or products* and to achieve specific *aims* and *benefits*. The project itself is simply a means to an end.

- Have an element of *uniqueness*. This emphasis distinguishes a project from a business process – where there is an emphasis on consistency. It is important not to push this factor too far as the trend to mass customization (and, for example, 1:1 marketing) emphasizes variety from business processes, and project-based organizations (consulting, engineering and others) emphasize consistency in projects.

- Have *resources*: for example, of people, money, equipment and *constraints* including targets related to time, cost and performance.

- Follow a *lifecycle* and contain stages. Each stage includes a number of activities and deliverables, and is typically completed by a phase-end milestone.

- Have a definite start and finish.

- Are complex.

- Involve uncertainty.

The nature and role of project management follows from the definition of a project. Project management is: 'planning, monitoring and controlling all aspects of a project and motivation of all those involved to achieve the project objectives on time and to the specified cost, quality and performance' (APM Body of Knowledge).

It is also helpful to see that there are many aspects to successful project management: 'projects do not succeed just by assiduous adherence to a mechanical process... successful projects are managed with enthusiasm, vision, single-mindedness and integrity' BS6079.

'Agile' approaches to projects have evolved in cultures where 'technical' skills are valued. These technical skills come in many forms and include the professional skills of end-user groups. In agile approaches, the emphasis is on success through people, creating an environment where multi-disciplinary teams can work together effectively delivering benefits through innovation and business change. The role of the project manager becomes leadership of a multi-disciplinary team of people with professional skills. The project manager as 'first among equals', often plays a facilitating role. In a sense, agile approaches are a reaction against traditional approaches, which can represent a hierarchical model with the project manager 'in charge'.

The 'agile manifesto' (Figure 5.1), written by a group of thought leaders in this area captures the key principles of an agile approach.

Agile Manifesto - Principles

We are uncovering better ways of developing software by doing it and helping others do it. Through this work we have come to value:

- Individuals and interactions over processes and tools.

- Working software over comprehensive documentation.

- Customer collaboration over contract negotiation.

- Responding to change over following a plan.

That is, while there is value in the items on the right, we value the items on the left more.

www.agilemanifesto.org

Figure 5.1: Agile manifesto

For many organizations, these principles represent a fundamental, radical shift from how they currently approach projects. We explore each principle in turn.

Individuals and interactions over processes and tools.

Projects can develop an emphasis on specific techniques, tools and deliverables. Huge effort is expended on interim deliverables, such as requirements and design *documents* which are simply a means to an end. Agile approaches emphasize people and their interactions. This is very clear in the practice of having a 'co-located' team – a team with a 'team room' to work in where they can communicate easily.

Working software over comprehensive documentation.

Agile approaches, with their foundation in IT development, focus on working software. They tackle technical issues and start development early in the lifecycle. This reflects the importance of working software as an output (rather than the design document). It also reflects that as people see early versions of working software they will have a better understanding of what they need and what is possible. This reflects the vale of prototypes and pilots of many kinds.

It is important not to see this as implying no documentation. The development is just not driven by documentation and documents are produced where they genuinely add value.

Customer collaboration over contract negotiation

Even within an organization, the relationship between business and IT functions can work in a formal, contractual style. This often reflects lack of trust. The extent of IT outsourcing also means that there are actual contractual relationships involved in many projects.

Given the inevitable uncertainty over requirements and the need for learning, this contractual emphasis is problematic. However, there are ways of setting contracts that at least begin to reflect the need for flexibility and close collaboration.

Agile approaches emphasize project teams working directly with the customer. This also removes much bureaucracy and accelerates the project process.

Responding to change over following a plan.

Agile approaches recognize that change is inevitable and seek to make it possible and cost effective. This is possible if project processes are kept simple and the strong technical skills in the team are used to establish a solution design that enables change.

An agile approach applies a shift in emphasis from *process* to *people* as the most important factor in succeeding with a project. The aim is to have *just enough* process. A well-managed agile project balances this focus on people and flexibility with maintaining discipline and control. Control is achieved with the minimum of additional work in a way that seeks to *add value* to the project, rather than adding effort and cost in seeking to comply with an externally imposed framework of controls. The key question to consider is: 'how does this activity help the team realize benefits?'

Building the team

The priority is to get the right people engaged in the core team and other roles. Then the goal is to create the right environment so they can work together effectively. You can't assume that this will just happen. Selecting the people and building a high performing team require considerable effort and attention. Again, the agile principles provide valuable guidance (Figure 5.2). It is also important to note that there is no single right way to structure the project team and governance framework.

Getting the right people is more than just getting the right job titles. It is getting the best mix of enthusiasts, critical friends, experts and idea generators.

Sharing the vision

There will almost certainly be new people joining the team at this stage. If it did not happen during the previous Explore stage, work on building the team will have to start.

It is vital to pay attention to ensuring the team has a clear understanding and commitment to the drivers and vision for the project. Do not leave this to chance or rely on them simply reading the benefits realization plan. This is a crucial 'hearts and minds' issue, which the sponsor should own. If the team members do not understand the reasons for the investment (drivers) and the high level goals (vision and investment objectives) they are unable to use their judgment effectively to drive innovation during the project, and the chances are the project will rapidly shift focus to technology delivery.

Agile Manifesto - Principles for agile IS development teams

Business people and developers must work together daily throughout the project.

Build projects around motivated individuals. Give them the environment and support they need, and trust them to get the job done.

The most efficient and effective method of conveying information to and within a development team is face-to-face conversation.

The best architectures, requirements, and designs emerge from self-organizing teams.

At regular intervals, the team reflects on how to become more effective, then tunes and adjusts its behavior accordingly.

Agile processes promote sustainable development. The sponsors, developers, and users should be able to maintain a constant pace indefinitely.

www.agilealliance.org

Figure 5.2: Details of the agile manifesto

Project roles and stakeholders

A stakeholder is anyone who has an interest in the outcome of a project. This includes both those responsible for the project and those affected by it.

Key stakeholders include:

- The project team.
- The project sponsor.
- The project board.
- End-users and customers.
- The expert technology partner.
- The project manager.

Team Design for Benefits Realization[T]

The project team that is put in place must be structured around the goal of realizing benefits from business change and must provide a foundation for effective teamwork and communication.

The project team members work together to deliver the objectives of the project. There will typically be a core team who work full time on the project and others who play key roles, but who are only part-time members of the team. As an example, specialist technical IT staff in the areas of networking or security may have to provide input to all projects.

The team model (Figure 5.3 & 5.4) provides a starting point for establishing a team for a specific project. The team can be as small as 3 people and there is no limit to the upper size, although keeping the team small is a key success factor. In practice, a team of more than 40-50 would be a very large agile project team.

It is essential that the six key roles are represented in the team from the start of the project, as the different perspectives and skills they bring all have a vital contribution.

The bulk of project resources are often in the development and test areas. However, in retail and banking scenarios, where there are many stores or branches, the deployment and training activities may require the majority of the resource allocated to the project.

Product or Benefit Lead

Works on behalf of the sponsor to ensure the realization of benefits for the organization. The role leads the benefits focus and will lead on business process and change issues.

Project Manager

The role of the project manager is to work with the team, and on behalf of the project sponsor to ensure the project is successful. This includes working with the team leads to deliver the project – to time, cost and performance priorities.

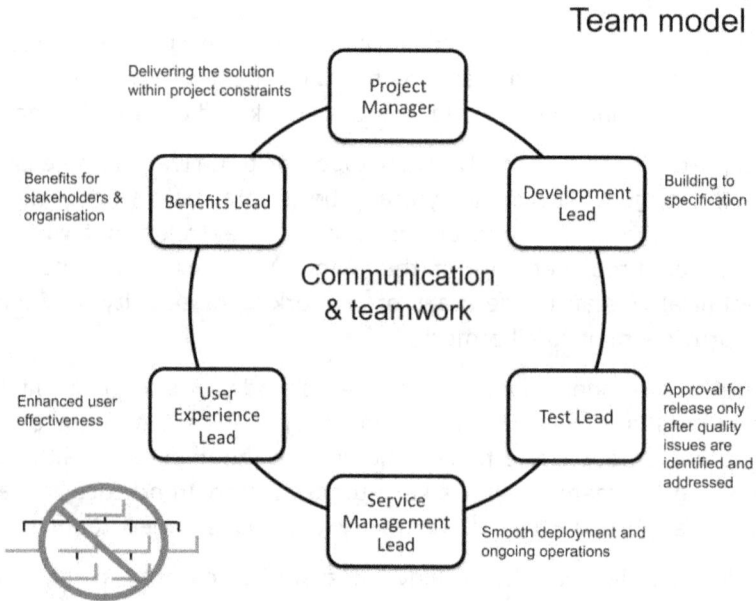

Team model

Figure 5.3: Project team model focused on benefits realization

User Experience Lead

Focuses on benefits for the end-user. The role includes usability and user education. Works very closely with the Benefits Lead on work design / business processes. This role often has the overall responsibility for communications strategy.

Development Lead

Responsible for development of the IT solution.

Test Lead

Responsible for testing of the IT solution and the wider business process / changes.

Service Management Lead

Responsible for the smooth transition of the system and new ways of working into the operational environment.

Figure 5.4: Team roles

The Product (or Benefits) Lead (focus: benefits for the organization) works very closely with the User Experience Lead (focus: benefits for the end user). The role includes:

- Understanding the marketplace and competition.

- Understanding the customer and what would add value to them.

- Responsibility for realizing benefits from the product / service over its lifetime.

- Phased delivery of the product / service to enable early benefits and understanding of the customer opportunity.

- Continued innovation and improvements to deliver value.

- Establishing performance measures to assess benefits and to drive learning and improvement.

- Working with a range of other disciplines to realize the potential benefits.

In many traditional projects, the project team structure and management style is very hierarchical. Communication channels are formal and the project manager may be the only one to speak to the Sponsor. The implicit model behind this approach is that 'the project manager knows best'.

An agile project requires a very different approach. There is a strong emphasis on teamwork, along with individual responsibility and empowerment, and open communication. Agile approaches are based on the belief that motivated individuals are key to successful projects and also that open communication between the different disciplines is essential for the identification and delivery of a successful business solution, particularly where there is a need for innovation.

Traditional approaches often focus on 'control': imposed 'top-down' on the team. Agile approaches emphasize 'discipline': the good practices established and owned by a motivated and skilled team.

There is no single best way to structure a project team. For a variety of reasons, apparently sensible people establish very strange structures for project 'teams'. *The team model provides a conceptual model for the roles required in a project team and can be used as a starting point when designing a team for a specific project.* In practice, it can be helpful to design the roles around the people - as well as find the people to fill the required roles. The challenge is to ensure that the overall team is effective. Team roles are likely to change and evolve during the project as the balance of different types of work changes and different strengths emerge and are required. Note that the split between the project roles and the ongoing responsibility for the service will vary from project to project.

The role of the architect

An important additional project role is that of Architect. The role can be implemented in a variety of ways depending on the size and skills of the team. It brings an overall focus on the capability and integrity of the business and technical solution. This involves looking beyond the project to programme and organizational level including, for example, ensuring appropriate compliance with technical standards and reuse of infrastructure services.

There are a number of aspects to the architecture role on a project relating to conceptual, logical and technical design. The logical design (solution architecture) provides the vital link between the business side of the solution (as represented by the Product Lead in the conceptual design) and the technology side (as represented by Development in the physical design). The knowledge and skills of the architect help to provide an understanding of what is possible and of the effort and risk of different options. The role helps to enable business innovation through exploiting features of the technology.

Figure 5.5: The role of the architect

The role of the 'architect' is not explicit in the team model, the role can be extremely valuable at project, programme and portfolio levels (Figure 5.5).

The project sponsor

The project sponsor has overall responsibility for the project on behalf of the organization. The primary objective of the role is to ensure the investment is successful and that the intended benefits are realized. The nature of the role will vary considerably depending on the nature and size of the project. It can be a significant, challenging role and may in some cases be full time.

The authority and credibility of the sponsor will often be critical in gaining support for the project and for making the required changes to the organization happen. The sponsor will often have to work with and influence senior business colleagues who are responsible for benefits and related changes.

Figure 5.6 provides an example of a role description for a project sponsor.

The role of a project sponsor in his own words.... "*My role as project exec was:*

- *Challenging of detailed reports.*
- *Co-ordination – handling tensions between different stakeholders, making it happen at board meetings and in between.*
- *'Coaching' outside the meeting* (e.g. other senior stakeholders).
- *Clarifying roles and making sure people worked as a team.*
- *Anticipating weak areas e.g. post implementation capacity to operate the system; I commissioned a report on knowledge transfer and post-live admin.*
- *Being sensitive to communications.*
- *Managing expectations*"

This "*took up a lot of time – a substantial number of hours each week for a year*". "*I gave him* (the project manager*) the support he needed*", he had "*daily contact with the project exec*".

Figure 5.6: The role of a project sponsor

The extent and type of involvement required from the sponsor will vary according to type of the project (See Figure 5.7). Too much executive involvement can be a bad thing (Support projects).

Leadership Roles for Different Types of Project

Strategic

A senior manager with credibility with the top management team must be actively involved with the project for all or a significant part of their time. The focus of the role is on alignment with strategy and maximizing the business opportunity from this innovative project.

Exploratory

The senior management role is primarily about creating a climate where Exploratory projects can happen.

There will be significant / credible business involvement in the project team (Product / Project Manager).

Core Operations

There is a significant requirement for senior operational management leadership. Focus areas will include ensuring involvement and support from the range of business areas affected, managing the business risks, ensuring a continued focus on benefits through the steering committee and milestone reviews.

Support

The senior management role focuses on ensuring that there is a clear business case for the project and the focus is on a 'good enough' (80-20) solution.

There may not be a need for significant ongoing involvement.

Figure 5.7: Leadership roles for different types of project

The project board

The project board is an important part of the overall management framework or 'governance' framework for projects. It provides a forum for the project sponsor and project manager to work with other key stakeholders in the project. The project board meets at the end of project stages and /or on a regular basis (two weekly / monthly) and takes major decisions on the project.

The composition of the project board will depend on many factors. On large projects, the project sponsor will need to include senior managers from other business areas to enable them to be involved in key project decisions. It also includes user representatives, a senior manager from the area(s) affected and a senior IT manager (a representative of the Chief Information Officer / IT Director and potentially the external supplier of software /services).

Some project managers find it helpful to establish other groups (vision or strategy group, user representatives) that allow the project board to focus on progress towards benefits against timescale and cost. The other groups provide a forum for exploration and communication of wider project issues.

End-user involvement

Getting the right level of user involvement is hard. In many organizations it is very difficult to release good people to be part of project teams – they are too valuable where they are.

Having made people available, getting them involved effectively is difficult. There is a tendency for projects to focus on technology issues and to use techniques and a 'language' that makes it hard for users to contribute. One of the advantages of a benefits-driven approach is to make a shift in language away from technology towards business issues.

It is important to think through what is required to enable people to work effectively as they become part of a project team. For example, what induction is required, or is any specific training relevant? In many cases, it would be valuable to include education to introduce and reinforce relevant aspects of the 'toolkit.'

There is also a balance to make between full-time involvement in the team of a small number of users and wider involvement of all, or part, of the wider user community. Users who become part of the project team may, paradoxically be treated as outsiders by their old team and not seen as *representatives* of end-user views or able to take decisions on behalf of end users.

It is helpful to recognize that in many cases there will be a significant learning process for individuals and teams during and following implementation. There is no way to eliminate this. Even with good and effective user involvement throughout the project, new users have to go through a learning process as part of training and deployment. The project needs the resources, time and focus to enable and support this learning process. In many cases this means significantly more than a one-off, 'press this button', training course.

It is important to recognize that there will be many different end user-viewpoints and different perspectives on the opportunities and requirements. Within a stakeholder group (defined by the benefits and changes involved) further segmentation may be valuable – for example, some users may be natural 'early adopters' and can be valuable in providing feedback and promoting adoption. The level of segmentation will often be increased as the project progresses. It is helpful to tailor the communication and engagement approach to the different segments.

The project manager

The role of the project manager is to work with the team, and on behalf of the project sponsor, to ensure the project is successful. This includes working with the team leads to:

- Deliver the project – to time, cost and performance priorities.

- Build, lead and motivate the project team throughout the project.

- Ensure work is allocated and responsibilities identified.

- Keep the sponsor and senior management informed of progress / problems.

- Recommend termination of the project, if justified.

- Ensure there is a focus on communication between the team, organization, suppliers, etc.

Effective teamwork and communication

Success of a project depends on the people involved. The effective teamwork of the project team and the engagement with wider stakeholders make the difference between success and failure.

The project team design must ensure ownership for:

- Effective teamwork– this should be the project manager or one of the team leads who has real commitment to this area and relevant experience.

- Communication with and involvement of stakeholders – the different project leads (and potentially other team members) should have responsibility for working with agreed stakeholders.

- Use of IT to enable communication and effective team working.

There are many other practices to consider: selection of team members; location of the team; team meetings, etc. See Further Reading for some good sources of further information.

Use of technology

Getting people communicating directly with others is a key part of an agile approach. If the team is working in the same workspace ('co-located') they can talk face to face or gather round a whiteboard to work on a problem. Diagrams on whiteboards and flip chart paper will be on the walls – providing a record of discussions and decisions and being there to refer to later. If the detail isn't clear, you can always ask the colleague who drew the diagram in the first place.

This approach eliminates huge efforts producing reports and documents that are largely there for compliance reasons - so that risk averse managers can refer to a paper trail when things go wrong. For the people doing the work their elimination is no loss – they probably didn't use them anyway.

Even in this environment of face-to-face discussion and simple diagrams on flipcharts and whiteboards, technology is important. Some documents are required. Some contributors to the project cannot work full time with the team. Core team members may have to travel as part of the project. A wide range of stakeholders need to be kept in touch and involved. Management need to be kept informed.

For all these reasons the team needs to be able to make effective use of IT to enhance their effectiveness as individuals and as a team, as well as their ability to communicate with broader stakeholders in the project.

There are a number of implications:

- The team needs someone who can provide a lead to ensure individuals and the team as whole is making effective use of IT. This can involve establishing agreed protocols for the use of email, phone and instant messaging, as well as talking to each other. It also involves the use of project management, intranet and portal solutions for team working and wider communication.

- There are practices for the toolkit here as well. These can form the basis for capturing and sharing learning and for enabling teams to get these aspects of the project working well as quickly as possible.

Get set for success: a strategic project

The project was a Strategic project and the project team was expected to grow to 12-15 people. There was a good work area where all the team members could be located but some element of mobile working was going to be involved (visiting customers and other stakeholders, working from home, etc). There were a number of project stakeholders within and outside the organization.

The project manager decided to keep responsibility for effective teamwork, partly to demonstrate its importance. She also arranged to bring in a specialist from the HR team to help with the project kick-off workshop and various other team-building activities.

The Sponsor took responsibility for communication with a number of the key business stakeholders. The Product Manager also had a specific role.

One of the two User Experience members of the team had specific experience of using a range of communication technologies and worked with the Project Manager to:

- Establish a team workspace and set up information management for the team (including handling of core documents, risk and issues logs, etc).

- Establish a project intranet site that provided information and a communication channel to stakeholders outside the core team.

- Establish an agreed communication etiquette for the team (e.g. how and when to use email, phone, face to face communication, etc).

- Provide guidance on the communication etiquette and use of the various technologies to team members.

- Ensuring there is time to reflect, learn and improve.

Figure 5.8: Approach to a strategic project – an example

Building the team: summary

Getting the right people engaged in all the different team and stakeholder roles is vital. There may be some tough decisions to take during the project to make changes if this is not right first time. In any case, structures and roles are likely to need to evolve during the project.

Delivering the change programme

The benefits realization plan helps to define what changes are required to realize the benefits. During Evolve, the focus shifts to actually delivering the change programme. The changes and the types of interventions required to realize them will be of many kinds. In this section, we explore a number of important aspects of successfully delivering the change programme.

See Further Reading for sources of more information on change management and software engineering.

Stakeholder Communications and Engagement[T]

Our focus on stakeholder engagement highlights the importance of the communications strategy and role. This is a vital part of benefits realization.

Who is being communicated with about what? When is communication required? What method should be used for each communication? These are all vital decisions. How to enable feedback and effective two-way communication is also an important element of the overall strategy.

In many cases one of the team leaders will take on the role of 'communications lead.' This will often be the User Experience Lead or Benefits Lead. The aim is to bring specific expertise in communication with stakeholders, and to support other team members as they engage with different stakeholders

Marketing perspectives and practices have an important contribution to make. Thinking about 'brand' and communicating the benefits to customers and other end-users may be critical in establishing adoption and usage.

Phased Deployment[T] and benefits ramp-up

Well executed waterfall and agile projects ensure that new business processes are defined alongside the system and are tested, along with training materials, as part of final user testing of the system. However, in many cases these effectively become frozen at this stage and even if there is a pilot deployment of the solution the pressure to complete deployment tends to prevent any significant changes:

> *"One engagement was deploying a solution to a number of countries in a phased rollout. However, the target dates meant that there was no time in the schedule to allow for any learning from the initial deployment to be incorporated in the planning."* (quote from a recent research project)

There is a major risk that business processes and training are frozen just as some of the most significant learning is taking place as the solution is deployed in the real world. It is important to build in genuine opportunities for learning about the potential benefits and how best to realize them as part of the deployment process.

As part of project planning, consideration is given to the extent of innovation in business process and working practices and the likely need for learning and change through a phased deployment. Business process documentation and training materials are tested as normal during user acceptance testing and there is a rapid pilot implementation.

The project team works closely with the pilot users to understand how best to realize benefits from the new systems and ways of working. Processes and training material are amended to reflect the learning – this is facilitated by their format, and a second phase of pilot deployment is carried out based on the revised training and business processes. When this is successful, widespread deployment is started. The learning process is maintained throughout the deployment.

Approaches to phased deployment: examples from recent research projects

Example 1

"Organizational structure, regardless of general belief, is not strong enough to set into motion significant transformations of processes and system operation, acting from a centralized position. It will be necessary, within the scope of project implementation, to go one-by-one through almost every single government body and talk to employees, organize short training, find Quick Win and Win Win possibilities and see how the solution can be implemented in the most efficient and quickest way."

Example 2

"One organization had implemented a groupware / document management solution. A 'top down' implementation approach had resulted in very little usage of the facilities. As a result, they invested in a 'bottom up' approach with an experienced user working with groups of users to establish how they might realize benefit from the new capabilities – and to support them in using the technology to improve ways of working."

Figure 5.9: Approaches to phased deployment

These projects effectively separated delivery of the software solution from deployment and continued the development of business processes and training through a series of phased deployment activities. The practice adopts an evolutionary approach, not a 'one shot' approach. This fits with the iterative, incremental approach to the software delivery and extends it to the overall business solution. The practice is based on a critical success factor of speed to benefits rather than speed to deployment of a technology solution.

Cut-over: implementation, training and education

At each stage of the deployment, detailed planning for implementation will be required as well as training and education aimed at different stakeholder groups. Even with the best designed systems and built in help, etc, this is often a major activity for the project team.

Training and education contribute to the implementation of organizational changes and is a major part of a project. Very often, there is underinvestment in this area. It is important to design the training with a benefits focus as part of the wider activity to realize benefits.

Benefits realization depends on business changes to introduce new ways of working (for example, a new business process) as well as one-off, enabling changes (for example, new roles). The impact of changes may be hard to predict and there may be unexpected results. It is important to monitor the impact of planned changes and to watch out for unexpected impacts.

It is likely that changes will continue after the new IT system goes live and after the project is completed. Resources for these changes and the handover of responsibility from the project team to operational management are important.

It is also important to design the training in such a way that changes during the life of the project can be accommodated effectively. There will be a need for continued provision of training to meet the needs of new staff as well as to enable continued learning and fuller exploitation of the system.

Many factors will influence the approach taken to implementation of the changes. The IT and Change portfolio is one important starting point for adapting the approach taken.

Summary: delivering the changes

Delivering the business changes required to realize the benefits is a vital element of the project. One guideline suggests that at least 50% of project budget should be allocated to these people-related activities.

The changes are complex and the results of actions can be unpredictable. It is vital that the sponsor, project team and other key stakeholders continue to focus on this area.

Planning and control

The foundations of a successful project are laid at the very early stages. It is also true that the seeds of failure are often sown at the beginning of a project. Many projects proceed when the problems that will emerge later and cause major problems or failure are clear to see. One major success factor for organizations is to stop failing projects and the best time to do this is right at the beginning, if possible before they start.

The emphasis during Engage and Explore has been on ensuring that there are clear goals for the project (defined in terms of benefits) and that these align with the needs of stakeholders and the strategy of the organization. This alignment is not so much about approval of a piece of paper (the benefits realization plan in this case) as a key group of people with a shared vision committed to making it happen.

We have restated key agile principles to provide a context and avoid a drift into process and control as an end in itself. Key practices, when used well, are there to ensure and accelerate progress towards the goals of benefits realization.

Agile Manifesto - Principles for an agile IS development process

Our highest priority is to satisfy the customer through early and continuous delivery of valuable software.

Welcome changing requirements, even late in development. Agile processes harness change for the customer's competitive advantage.

Deliver working software frequently, from a couple of weeks to a couple of months, with a preference to the shorter timescale.

Working software is the primary measure of progress.

Continuous attention to technical excellence and good design enhances agility.

Simplicity--the art of maximizing the amount of work not done--is essential.

www.agilealliance.org

Figure 5.10: Further aspects of the agile manifesto

This section addresses a number of aspects of project planning which build on the benefits foundations already established:

- The project framework – he detailed aspects of the Evolve stage.

- Work breakdown structure.

- Estimating.

- Living documents

- Governance framework.

- Benefits-driven change control.

- Risk management.

- Milestone review.

- Aspects of the project plan and project planning.

Project framework – milestones and deliverables

The e^{4+1} project framework provides a broad framework that is suitable for many types of projects. It has been designed specifically to start before traditional projects and to capture ideas and manage them as projects from the beginning. It also goes beyond the completion of traditional projects with Evaluate and Expand, to take a benefits perspective on post-project review and focus on developing the benefits being realized. As a result, much of traditional project activity is within one phase of e^{4+1} – Evolve. Therefore, it is helpful to consider how Evolve can itself be broken down into a series of stages with clear deliverables and milestones. This is particularly important for larger projects.

The same arguments apply for the value of this approach as for the e^{4+1} framework overall. There is considerable benefit for each project and for the management of projects across the organization to have an element of standardization. The benefits of reuse and shared learning are significant. There is also plenty of scope for each project team to adapt the approach to their needs.

The table sets out an example based on the Microsoft Solutions Framework (MSF). MSF is a very effective framework and was an important source of inspiration and ideas for aspects of the book. Although developed before 'agile' became fashionable it embodies many of the same principles.

Project Lifecycle: Stage – Milestone – Deliverables

Envisioning: Vision and scope approved

- Benefit plan / business case
- Technology validation
- Vision and scope (needs, options, statement of requirements) [this could be referred to as the Project strategy]
- Project structure
- Risk assessment

Planning: Project plan approved

- Project plan and project schedule
- Communications strategy
- Functional specification
- Solution design

Developing: Scope complete

- Solution code
- Draft training materials
- Draft documentation: deployment processes, operational procedures, support and troubleshooting
- Marketing materials

Stabilizing: Release readiness

- Release-ready versions of: source code and executables, end-user help and training materials, operations documentation

Deploying: Deployment complete

- New systems and ways of working operational
- Benefits review and action plan

Figure 5.11: Project lifecycle

Notes: Envisioning (see the table) is broadly equal to Explore; all other stages are part of Evolve. Within Developing, which is the primary focus of software development (but preliminary work may well take place earlier), there will be a number of interim milestones and software releases, for example, every 2 weeks. In addition, the team would follow what is now a common agile practice, of a daily build and test cycle, which provides continuous feedback on the emerging system. A major implication, as already noted, is that key skill areas have to be represented throughout the life of the project.

Work breakdown structure

Establishing a work breakdown structure (WBS) is an important early step in project planning. The project manager and team start with the high level goals of the project and identify the 'products' or deliverables and the major activities required as part of the project in order to achieve the goals. At its lowest level, the WBS should show tasks that can be allocated to an individual and completed in one progress-reporting period (typically a week – though potentially a day at key stages and in some agile methods). The WBS should be developed by the project team leads and team members, taking into account their expertise. There will usually be a need to reconcile the WBS with expectations set by management.

The WBS provides a basis for controlling the project, for resource planning, for estimating effort, elapsed time and cost, and provides a valuable input to risk identification.

Some agile approaches argue that the work breakdown structure should be discarded, arguing instead for a list of features and an evolving, bottom-up estimate of effort required from the developers. While we support the importance of estimates being made and owned by the people who will do the work, we consider that the WBS still has a role to play, perhaps at a high level in giving a basis for the project plan, particularly the many aspects that are not directly related to software development. We also note that our emphasis on phased delivery, benefits-driven trade-offs and milestone-based control bring a strong dynamic for the project, very different from a bottom-up, task-based plan driven from the WBS.

Estimating

Estimating the effort and cost of a project is a key element in planning. In many cases, developing a business case is the first activity and is a prerequisite for getting people allocated to the project and starting work.

Establishing estimates of effort, duration and cost are a key part of project planning. There are two basic approaches – 'top-down' and 'bottom-up'. Both approaches are normally required. A 'top down' estimate is based on a broad understanding of the scope and complexity of the project. The estimate comes from comparing the project to other similar projects. The 'bottom up' estimate is developed by establishing a WBS and then estimating effort / duration / costs for activities at the lowest level on the WBS. An overall project estimate is then established simply by adding up the individual estimates. The top-down and bottom-up estimates are compared and an overall estimate for the project negotiated and agreed.

The agile approach focuses on estimates for specific features ('user stories') and the allocation of features to a series of internal releases provides focus and flexibility. The team will get better at estimating during the project based on their shared experience so that there should be increased confidence in the delivery of later releases.

Estimating is an art not a science and a number of elements of the approach to projects address the inevitable uncertainty in the initial estimates and budgets. The practice of making benefits-driven trade-offs is important, as the one thing we do know about the estimate is that it will not be 100% accurate.

Living documents

The production of documents on a project (requirements, plans, designs, etc) can become an end in itself. It is easy to lose site of the fact that these documents are only a means to an end – the goal of providing benefits to stakeholders. In particular, there can be huge effort involved in getting a document 'just right' because this is (often correctly) seen as the last chance to make changes, for example, to requirements. This causes extra effort and delay. It also prevents learning and change.

An agile approach seeks to 'maximize the amount of work *not done*' – in part by eliminating and streamlining documentation deliverables. There is still considerable documentation required and the Living Documents practice addresses how this is produced.

The approach of 'baseline early – freeze late' is used. Many aspects of a deliverable can often be captured quickly (80:20 rule). This can be 'base-lined' and brought under change control while further work is done. This allows other parts of the project to proceed. For example, it avoids excessive delays that can result if the project attempts to ensure requirements and specifications are fully complete and locked down before development start. The deliverable is kept under change control and is frozen as late as possible.

The standard project framework also means that effort is saved and quality is improved by using templates for key deliverables and by reusing sections that address aspects of the project approach that do not need to vary (much) from project to project.

Business Change Governance Framework[T]

We have already discussed a number of important elements of the governance framework: the role of the sponsor; project team and project board. The governance framework is designed to meet the needs of the specific situation, take account of key individuals and what they can contribute, and specifically to address IT-enabled business change rather than technology delivery. The business focus means that benefits owners should be included in the framework as members of the project board, for example.

The key thing to focus on is that effective governance is really about behavior not structure. Do the senior managers actually turn up or do they send deputies? Does action take place outside project board meetings so that the meetings themselves can be effective? Is there shared ownership for solving problems or is it a game of politics? Is there willingness to learn and adapt as the project progresses?

When we work with projects, these issues of leadership and behavior really make the difference. Even where there is a good governance framework on paper, there are often problems in practice. The project sponsor and manager have important roles in ensuring the governance framework works effectively.

A colleague referred to the governance framework as providing the heartbeat of the project. For example, if the main project meeting is monthly and nobody has done much follow through between meetings the heartbeat is very slow. If the agile practice of daily meetings is adopted maybe the heartbeat is racing – but that is ok – for limited periods. A combination of a focused daily or weekly meeting with project board meetings at regular milestones (roughly every 4 weeks) is often a good way to drive progress.

Example of a governance framework for a Strategic project

The key elements of the governance framework for a Strategic project included:

- Weekly progress reports (brief) from each sub-team.

- Weekly team leads meeting with the project manager and sponsor.

- Fortnightly risk meeting (team leads and others).

- Milestone-based steering committee meetings involving all benefits owners at the end of each project phase (no phase lasting longer than 4-6 weeks).

- Regular meetings with key stakeholders.

In addition, milestone reviews were carried out and there was a range of activities to communicate with / involve wider stakeholder groups (end-users, help desk, etc).

Figure 5.13: Example of a governance framework

It is vital to drive towards progress as determined by the milestone targets, as this will ensure momentum and innovation. Don't just meet and see how things are going! Now that may seem common sense – but we would not have to mention it if it was already common practice – look very hard at the effectiveness of the project board on your current projects(s), for example.

Benefits-Driven Change Control[T]

Change is inevitable. In fact, change can often be a positive response to learning about new opportunities for benefits during a project. Control of change is an important discipline and has formed part of traditional project and systems development methods.

Too much change can mean that a project never delivers. Completely preventing change is unrealistic as there will always be learning during the course of a project and this may be significant. Particularly in scenarios where the benefits arise from innovation rather than incremental change, there will be a creative process of learning and discovery as possibilities are explored. The change control process needs to evaluate change requests and decide if action is required in the current or a future release. For example, the incremental approach means that delivery dates are only changed as a last resort, but within and between releases there is flexibility in the specific features that are prioritized for delivery.

Benefits driven change control builds on a traditional approach to change control and ensures that changes are evaluated primarily on the basis of their impact on benefits (rather than software features).

Change control example from recent research

The project sponsor worked with the project manager to establish a benefits-driven framework for change control. A contingency of 15% of the project budget was set aside as a provision for changes and other contingencies. This contingency was to be managed by the project board. If additional funds were required, approval would depend on normal financial approval processes.

Figure 5.14: Example of change control

There is a tendency to subject requests for changes to very high levels of scrutiny, often beyond that applied to the original business case. The change control framework must not be too onerous or it will result in important changes not being progressed or the change control system being by-passed.

Risk Management[T]

Risk management is a critical project activity and should be an ongoing process throughout the project. It is important to balance the effort given to this area – work is required to identify possible risks and to take *action*. Often organizational politics or some form of organizational blindness can mean it is very difficult to get agreement to action.

We advocate a simple approach to risk management on the basis that actively managing risks is the goal and that there is little value added by attempting to get too precise in the quantification of probability or financial impact.

Where an organization has an established approach to risk management it is probably most effective to keep using it. Just check how effectively it is being used and if the risks are being considered in relation to benefits realization rather than technology delivery.

Active management of risks

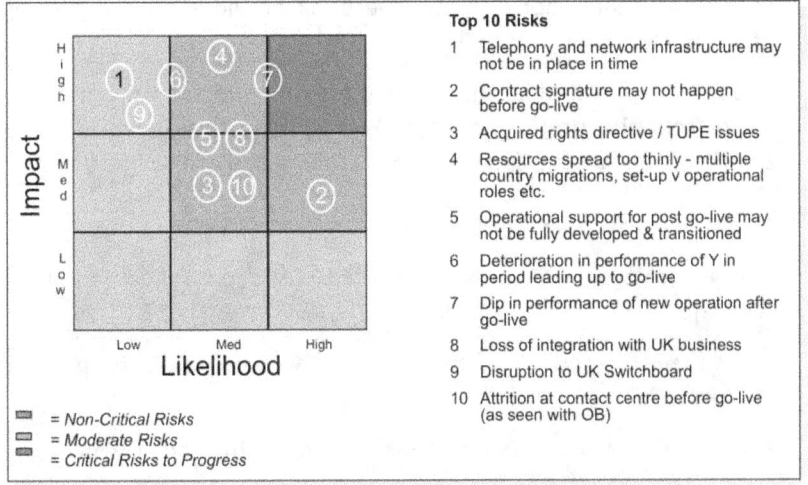

Top 10 Risks

1   Telephony and network infrastructure may not be in place in time
2   Contract signature may not happen before go-live
3   Acquired rights directive / TUPE issues
4   Resources spread too thinly - multiple country migrations, set-up v operational roles etc.
5   Operational support for post go-live may not be fully developed & transitioned
6   Deterioration in performance of Y in period leading up to go-live
7   Dip in performance of new operation after go-live
8   Loss of integration with UK business
9   Disruption to UK Switchboard
10 Attrition at contact centre before go-live (as seen with OB)

= Non-Critical Risks
= Moderate Risks
= Critical Risks to Progress

For each risk consider:

- Mitigating actions (to reduce the probability or impact).
- Contingency actions: what to do if it the risk happens.
- Ownership for the actions.
- When to review.

Figure 5.15: Risk management example

Milestone review

Management focus should be on the major milestones (stage ends) determined by the project lifecycle. If the project is kept short (as it should be) this will typically provide a major review point every 2-6 weeks, which becomes a motivating target for the project team and for the sponsor and project board, reducing the risk of slippage between milestones.

The deliverables at each milestone should be clearly defined. In some organizations, a standard lifecycle is defined with the same stages and major deliverables for each project. We strongly recommend this approach and the book provides an example of a lifecycle framework.

Each milestone is also an opportunity to reflect on progress and *learn* from the project to date. We address this Benefits Review activity in our discussion of the Evaluate stage of the lifecycle.

Milestone review: key questions

Have we achieved our goals for this stage? (Are specific deliverables complete?)

Are we ready to proceed to the next stage with resources and plans in place?

Are we still on track to deliver benefits that justify the project?

Is the risk assessment up to date and have appropriate actions been planned or taken?

What have we learned that will enable us to work more effectively in future stages and how are we going to make it happen?

Figure 5.16: Milestone review – key questions

The project plan

Project planning is an ongoing process throughout the project. Plans are updated and changed as the project progresses. Typically, there will be a high level plan for the overall project and a detailed plan for the current and next stage.

The project plan is far more than a timetable. It needs to address a range of questions:

- Why – is the project being undertaken?

- What – are the aims and target benefits?
- Who - is involved in delivering the benefits?
- What - is the business solution required?
- When – will the project be completed?
- How – will the project be carried out?

At the early stages of the project, this may be a one or two page document. As the project progresses it may become a much more substantial document. According to the preferences of the organization, a range of specific areas will have to be addressed either in sub-plans or as part of the overall document (Figure 5.18).

Aspects of the project plan and strategy

Communications and user engagement strategy

Security strategy

Test strategy

Deployment strategy

Training plan

Cut-over plan

Trade-off strategy

Milestones and deliverables

Figure 5.18: Aspects of the project plan

Trade-off strategy

The trade-off strategy should be made explicit as part of the plan. In most cases, the timescale is key and a small team works to deliver a release to the timetable. Resourcing might evolve during the project but the primary decision is to take a time-boxed approach and treat features as the key variable. The design needs to enable features to be moved from release to release, if required, to enable the implementation timescales to be met.

Figure 5.19 shows a typical agile approach to trade-offs. Resources are fixed (small teams are effective and adding people in response to problems is often not effective), a schedule (timescale) is chosen and then features are adjusted to enable the team to deliver to the timescale.

The trade-off matrix is an early agreement made
between the team and stakeholders

	Fixed	Chosen	Adjustable
Resources	✓		
Schedule		✓	
Features			✓

Given fixed RESOURCES, we will choose a SCHEDULE,
and adjust FEATURES as necessary.

Figure 5.19: Trade-off strategy for a typical agile (time-boxed) project

Planning and control: key factors

Many of the practices for project planning are similar for all
projects. When the goal is business innovation and benefits
enabled by IT the main difference is the 'mindset' (principles) with
which planning is approached.

The agile principle is critical: 'Simplicity--the art of maximizing the
amount of work **not** done.' Remember that a lot of project
processes are about the perception of control and are designed to
keep nervous management, who do not trust their teams, happy.
Discipline and control are essential, but focus should be on how
they can add value and contribute to effective progress towards
benefits realization (Figure 5.20).

Discipline v control

"Simplicity--the art of maximizing the amount of work not done--is
essential"

This agile principle provokes an instant negative reaction in many places,
yet it is at the heart of the approach. Our view is that high
performance teams are highly motivated and highly disciplined. They will
adopt and follow good practices that help them succeed. As highly
skilled knowledge workers, what will not work well is management

controls imposed on them that they perceive as adding effort, but not value, and hindering them in their mission.

Your job as a manger, or team member, is to be very clear how any element of work will help. Now this does NOT mean that we are against prototyping, exploration and the 'focused chaos' of an innovative project.

Figure 5.20: Discipline vs. control

Enabling learning and flexibility

A traditional approach to projects emphasizes the cost of making changes to the desired results or products that are the outcome of the project. The costs of making changes increases as the project continues. For example, at the start of a project changing requirements is only a matter of changing a list of bullet points in a Word document. Towards the end of the project, it could require changes to software, training materials and user procedures, as well as significant testing of the solution. The fact that the cost of change rises rapidly (exponentially) means that:

- Approaches to projects place a huge emphasis on planning, and trying to avoid the need for change. This may extend to preventing changes even if they are important.

- Managing and controlling change is a critical element of project management.

- Reducing the cost of change is in a sense the 'holy grail' of project management.

Traditional approaches to project management respond to this with a huge focus on planning – trying to get it right first time and on controlling (preventing) change. An element of 'agile' approaches to project management is to recognize that change is inevitable and should be welcomed. The agile response is to *enable* learning and change and to manage the project to reduce the cost of change.

Enabling business innovation

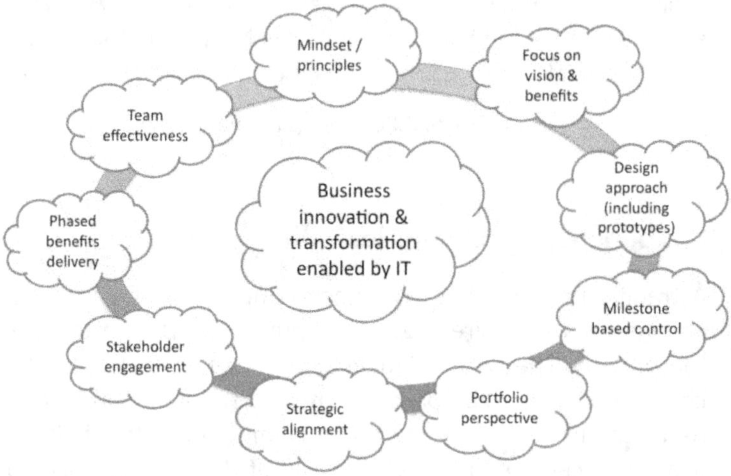

Figure 5.21: Aspects of an environment to encourage business innovation enabled by IT

e^{4+1} is designed to enable learning and flexibility, recognizing that change is not only inevitable but are desirable. A number of practices come together in e^{4+1} to create the possibility of learning and innovation during a project: the different disciplines involved in the team; the focus on phased benefits delivery (versioned release / incremental development); and the approach taken to project trade-offs, for example (Figure 5.21).

Making it happen – challenges

The shape of the Evolve stage will vary significantly from project to project; for example, is it a bespoke development, a package implementation or is it exploitation of elements of the existing IT infrastructure? The guiding principles and key practices remain the same. Inevitably experience and judgment will determine how they are applied in the specific situation.

In reviewing how projects are managed, and in planning changes and improvements, it is important to adopt the agile principle that activity on a project should contribute to the successful delivery of project goals and should not simply be for compliance purposes. A number of other factors are important:

- There is significant value from doing the basics consistently and well.

- There is 'no single best way' to approach a project. The approach taken should be adapted to reflect the context and the people in involved (within an overall consistent framework).

- Focus on the importance of people at all levels - both the project team and wider stakeholders and the need to establish a common vision and way of working.

- The importance of a clear guiding vision for the project team and related stakeholders. Often this is reinforced by clear and simple definition of key benefits and related measures.

- Leadership of the project – including the contribution of the sponsor and project manager. The role they play and the example they set will have a significant impact.

- The management of the overall portfolio and an enabling organizational climate that allows risk taking and encourages innovation and learning.

It is important to take a phased approach to improving the approach taken to projects. In many cases, there will be established good practices to build on and specific practices from this book can be gradually adopted.

In summary

Evolve is the core of the project where the ideas and plans are brought to life.

We have seen how many organizations approach projects and observed a wide range of strengths and weaknesses. Many are competent at traditional projects but struggle when innovation is required. Others are effective at technology delivery but cannot effectively tackle IT-enabled organizational change. Many waste months drifting from idea, through business case into project.

Most switch attention to the *next* project far too quickly rather than continuing to focus on realizing the benefits from the investment they have already made.

In virtually every case, a critical area for improvement is to develop the skills of the people involved to work together effectively. The issue is rarely technical skills. Projects are challenging; they require complex multi-disciplinary teamwork, which requires high-level skills in many areas. These need to be developed over time and require education, and ongoing support in an enabling environment.

***

6 Taking it further: Evaluate

Key topics covered in this chapter:

- o   *Evaluate is about carrying out a Benefits Review to assess the benefits realized, the opportunities for further benefits and any general lessons learned.*

- o   *The core Benefits Review practice can, and should, be applied at each stage of the lifecycle.*

- o   *A key objective is to act on learning and we make use of the ideas of the Learning Organization and 'knowing-doing gap' to explore how to make this happen.*

- o   *Team members gain valuable experience which contributes to the success of future projects.*

- o   *The use of practices and patterns as the foundation for a benefits toolkit to share good practices for benefits-driven projects.*

Why bother?

Is there any point carrying out a *benefits review*? Why not just call the project a success and move on to the next project or job? Is that not what usually happens?

Post-implementation reviews are not consistently carried out in most organizations. As a result, a major opportunity for learning is lost. In the minority of cases where a post implementation review is carried out, it is often soon after the IT solution goes live and focuses principally on the success of the IT solution delivery.

The benefits review builds on this and has an explicit focus on benefits. As a result, the gap between 'going live' and the review has to be extended to provide time for benefits to be established. In some cases follow up reviews are required to assess the benefits, for example, at the year-end or 12 months after the project.

The agile manifesto brings a still broader focus – which we adopt here:

> "At regular intervals, the team reflects on how to become more effective, then tunes and adjusts its behavior accordingly"

www.agilemanifesto.org

Benefits review becomes an ongoing process throughout the project with the Evaluate stage providing a major focus.

Planning and Carrying out the Benefits Review[T]

A broad guideline is that those who participate in a benefits review are most likely to learn lessons from the project. The best way of sharing the lessons with other projects is often moving team members on to be part of new project teams when the time is right.

The organizational culture can have a major effect on the ability to carry out reviews and their success. In many organizations admitting there is anything to learn is still hard and also personnel move so quickly from role to role there can be a lack of continuity between planning the project and reviewing the benefits.

The benefits review is intended to enable learning from success and failure (and avoid repeating mistakes), and increase the benefits realized from IT investments. Specific objectives are:

- To understand any changes in the business context or learning during the project that have an impact on the intended benefits.

- To identify the intended benefits that have been achieved.

- To identify the intended benefits that have *not* been achieved, the reasons why, and decide if any action to enable their realization is appropriate.

- To identify the benefits that have been achieved that were not expected.

- To identify any dis-benefits that have arisen and decide on any action to deal with them.

- To identify any further benefits which can now be obtained and agree if action should be taken realize them. (At some point projects reach the 80:20 point and resources should be reallocated to achieve bigger returns elsewhere.)

- To understand what types of benefits can be achieved and to determine the causes of success and failure, in order to provide better insight for other projects at the benefits planning stage.

- To better understand how the benefits management process works, and hence to be able to improve the process.

[Based on Ward J and Murray P (2000) *Benefits Management Best Practice Guidelines.* Information Systems Research Centre – Cranfield School of Management]

The review should involve key project stakeholders and should be based on relevant evidence. It is important to design and facilitate a workshop session that enables different stakeholders to contribute. In some cases it will be valuable to run a number of different sessions with individual stakeholder groups. The example describes one effective approach we have taken to running a benefits review session.

Example: approach to a Benefits Review workshop

The sponsor called key team members representing different stakeholders together for a 2-hour workshop. A facilitator, not connected with the project, was lined-up and a member of the team was asked to work as 'documenter' – typing the discussion and findings during the workshop.

The workshop started with a brief introduction to the purpose and objectives. The participants were asked to discuss: why did the project need to be undertaken? And: 'what were the overall objectives?'

Participants were then asked: 'what were the outcomes (benefits / dis-benefits)?' These were quickly explored by considering if the benefits were as planned and what unexpected benefits there had been.

Then the participants were asked to take some time thinking individually and writing on large post-its: what practices had worked well - and where are the opportunities for improvement. They were asked to consider before, during and, finally, after the project.

After about 10 minutes, each participant put their post-its on the wall one-by-one briefly explaining the point and gradually filling a rough 2*3 matrix. This allowed everybody to speak and make his or her contribution.

The facilitator followed up with questions to explore the major points made and to try and explore the underlying causes and opportunities for action.

Getting a shared focus on five priority areas for action and exploring what to do in each area wrapped up the session.

As the discussion was documented during the meeting, a draft report was issued for feedback the same day.

***

Note: as part of exploring each key issue it is important to consider if any problems are to do with lack of compliance with existing policy and frameworks, or if there is a need for new or changed policy and practice. It is also important to think hard about the underlying causes – keep asking 'why'?

Figure 6.1: Example of an approach to a Benefits Review

It is important to note that, as with risk management, reflection and learning should be an ongoing activity. The core benefits review carried out at the Evaluate stage of the lifecycle can be adapted for use during other stages of the project. The core of the practice is the same – the specific questions just need to be adapted slightly to the relevant stage of the project (Figure 6.2).

Project stage and the focus of benefits review

Engage

Is the opportunity worth investigating further?

Are we ready to develop the benefits realization plan?

Explore

Is there a clear benefits realization plan?

Is everything in place to proceed with the project?

Evolve

Milestone reviews at each stage: are we on track to realize benefits? (Note we expect the target benefits may change due to learning during the project)

The milestone review also considers:

- Have planned deliverables been completed?
- Is everything in place for the next stage of the project?
- Has the risk assessment been updated?
- Lesson learned that could help increase the effectiveness of project activity.

Evaluate

Benefits review: what benefits were realized (planned and unplanned)? What further benefits can be realized? What lessons can be learned for future projects?

Expand

Benefits review – periodic review of the production service: how can we sustain and improve benefits?

Figure 6.2: approach to Benefits Review at different stages of the lifecycle

Effective measurement of benefits

'You get what you measure' – performance measurement is a strong driver of behavior. As a result, the measures that are put in place and the targets that are set will have a significant impact on the benefits that are actually realized. Measurement is not just about assessing the results – measurement makes things happen.

Unfortunately, it is hard to predict the precise impact of specific measurements and there are often unexpected effects.

Measuring what is easy to measure may not be the right thing to do. Getting the data to measure what really matters can be difficult.

Effective measurement?

The supermarket was getting long queues of customers at the checkouts on a regular basis. One step they took to address this was to focus on the performance of checkout staff. From the new EPOS system they were able to measure 'items scanned per minute' so they introduced a daily report in each store showing the performance of each operator on each shift.

Performance of checkout operators increased.

However, the store manager saw that there was still a problem. The system was only measuring one part of the whole checkout process: the time between the scanning of the first and last item for each customer. Checkout operators were scanning the goods so rapidly that the shoppers couldn't keep up with the packing. There was a big pile of shopping at the end of the belt – with the customer frantically trying to pack it into bags – and the checkout operators were sitting waiting for the next customer – doing nothing.

So, they decided to experiment with a different set of measures...

Figure 6.3: Effective measurement

Having identified benefits and associated measures it is important to consider the likely impact of the individual measures, and the overall set of measures on behavior.

The Balanced Scorecard concept (see Further Reading) indicates that we need a 'basket' of measures, which together bring the right emphasis on behavior. Consider a sales role:

- A measure based on orders taken would be a starting point. But, by itself, what behavior might it drive?
- Other measures required might include:

  - Credit notes and bad debts (to assess what income was actually received).

  - Repeat business (as an indicator of customer satisfaction).

  - Order accuracy (problems highlighted by manufacturing).

Effective measurement is difficult. It comes into focus during the development of the benefits realization plan and should remain a focus during the project. Very often measures will need to evolve over time to shift the emphasis as different opportunities come into focus. A particular problem, and opportunity, is that often there is no effective measurement of the situation *before* the project: the project itself produced the capability to start to measure. Do not use this as an excuse to do nothing, or to spend a lot of time or money creating a baseline simply so you can measure the benefits more accurately. Keep the focus of activity on creating value.

Sharing the learning

Succeeding in implementing actions based on the learning from a benefits review is another major challenge. Research suggests that the rate of conversion from opportunities identified to *action taken* and improvements made is low. One of the best ways to learn is for an individual to be part of a benefits review session. In addition, as individuals move onto other projects they are likely to take their learning with them.

We want to explore two different perspectives which help us understand how to share learning and put it into practice. In an article and book about the Learning Organization, David Garvin (1993, 2000) refers to three overlapping stages of organizational learning:

- Cognitive: members of the organization are exposed to new ideas, expand their knowledge and begin to *think* differently.

- Behavioral: employees begin to internalize new insights and alter *behavior.*

- Performance improvement: changes in behavior lead to measurable *performance improvement.*

We need learning at all three stages. Garvin defines a **Learning Organization** as an organization skilled at *creating, acquiring, interpreting, transferring* and *retaining knowledge* and at *purposefully modifying* its *behavior* to reflect new knowledge and insights" (Garvin, 2000). This is an important element of our overall benefits realization capability – to purposefully modify behavior. He goes on to identify a number of enablers of learning:

- Create the opportunity to learn from all experiences – both good and bad – admit to failures.

- Foster an environment that is conducive to learning - make time to really understand customer needs, to think and reflect.

- Open up boundaries and stimulate the exchange of ideas.

- Create learning forums - reviews of strategy or cross-functional processes, including internal benchmarking.

A second perspective on learning is provided by Pfeffer and Sutton (1999) who refer to the gap between what we know and what we do. This 'knowing-doing' gap is a serious issue in the arena of IT-enabled change, as many valuable and widely known practices are not effectively adopted. The lack of adoption of the practice of carrying out a post-implementation review (benefits review) is just one of many examples.

Pfeffer and Sutton suggest that a major reason for the gap is that education and development focus on 'know-what' (to do) rather than 'know-why' (the underlying principles) and 'know-how' (the skills built up from experience of putting the knowledge into practice).

It is clear that although we can have valuable benefits review sessions the results will be limited if we do not take purposeful action to follow them up. Learning can be shared in a number of ways and this has to be planned and managed (Figure 6.1).

Examples of approaches to sharing learning

Updating policy and evolving the project framework (i.e. making change in the formal organization).

- Introduce a specific project lifecycle framework (such as e^{4+1}).
- Introduce a 'product manager' role into project teams.
- Focus project board activity on milestone reviews.

Capturing and sharing reusable resources

- A communications strategy (or other deliverables relating to the approach to the project) may be highly reusable.

Capturing aspects of tacit knowledge

- A project team has a 'brown bag' session (open workshop over lunch) to share their experience in a specific area.
- The team writes a short case study / prepares a podcast.
- Learning is captured as a new 'practice' to add to the toolkit.

Sharing knowledge through people

- Key players from the project are moved into other teams specifically with the goal of sharing their experience of new ways of working.

Training and education

- Standard courses are updated to reflect learning.
- A course is provided to introduce an agile, benefits-driven approach to projects.
- Education is provided in specific areas identified as priorities.

Experiments

- An agile approach is piloted on an Exploratory project using an external coach to support the new way of working.

Reward and recognition

- The CIO uses regular departmental briefings to recognize innovators.

Using networks

- Staff are encouraged to participate in external professional networks and attend conferences – with an emphasis on bringing back ideas to share with colleagues.

Figure 6.4: Approaches to sharing learning

The role of the Toolkit[T]

Background

Earlier in the book, we provided a brief introduction to patterns. We now make some links to thinking about knowledge management and organizational learning.

Thinking on *patterns* has developed from a number of sources including the work of Alexander (1977) in architecture. In essence, a pattern is an outline of 'what works' based on observation of practice. Software developers have adopted the concept of 'patterns' and more recently patterns have been used by those interested in software development processes and IT education.

From an IT development perspective, Nandhakumar and Avison (1999) highlight the limitations of formal methodologies which often represent only a *'convenient fiction'*, to provide an appearance of control, but bear little relationship to how work actually gets done: the methodology represents a focus on the formal process rather than the actual *practices* that relate to how people do their work. Brown and Duguid (see Chapter 4) provide a similar critique of business process re-engineering.

Practices and patterns

Practice is an increasingly widely used term, and a range of descriptions and definitions have emerged. Wenger suggests the following definition: *'a set of socially defined ways of doing things in a specific domain: a set of common approaches and shared standards that create a basis for action, problem solving, performance and accountability'*.

Not only does the concept of a practice appear to be very closely aligned with how people actually work, it is also particularly relevant in knowledge-intensive activities, such as IT projects, where much of the effort is based upon the experiences of individual and teams. Moreover, the concept of practice relates to the informal organization and how work is *actually* done by individuals and groups.

For our purposes, we have made the following distinction:

- A *practice* relates to an approach to getting work done in a specific context. Some authors refer to practices as 'routines.' Practices are what people *do* within your organization

- A *pattern* is an abstraction, a description of a practice. It must lose some of the richness and uniqueness of the related practice but it provides a way to identify and communicate what works. We have used the concept of patterns as a basis for the benefits-driven toolkit for IT-enabled change.

In this book we have provided brief outlines of some of the tools to contribute to the adoption of the specific ideas. The of 'tools' and the format of a 'pattern' provides a valuable way for an organization to approach capturing and sharing good practices identified locally.

Practices, knowledge management and organizational learning

An important strand of thinking about knowledge management is the distinction between explicit and tacit knowledge. This categorization of knowledge as either explicit or tacit is likely to be misleading: there are different levels of tacit knowledge and of skills. In some cases, important aspects of tacit knowledge can be made explicit while retaining much of its value. For example, some 'tacit skills could be articulated readily if organizational members were simply asked the question 'how do you do that?' (Ambrosini and Bowman, 2001)

Thompson and Walsham (2004) showed that if knowledge is to remain useful once made explicit, a link with the *context* in which the knowledge was used and so in which it might be reused must be retained. They also noted that while the ideal of 'strictly explicit knowledge is self contradictory' there are still opportunities to codify some aspects of knowledge that will be useful, particularly with a specific context as provided by, for example, a community of practice. Kamoche et al. (2003) use the jazz metaphor of improvisation in suggesting that there is an 'optimal amount of structure'.

The jazz analogy is that skilled professionals, whether jazz musicians or people engaged in a multi-disciplinary team to deliver IT-enabled change, need some common understanding to work together. This is not a score to follow note by note but a common language; common ways of working provide by the benefits principles and toolkit.

The tension between codifying nothing, thereby risking the loss of important information, and trying to codify everything, risking banality, is at the very core of attempts at knowledge management.

The codification of practice into knowledge is of its essence an active and social task 'connecting people so that they can think together' (Alvesson and Karreman, 2001), bringing together different people with different experience and enabling them to contribute their knowledge in a team (Becker, 2001). The goal is to enable group learning by the 'sharing of individual interpretations to develop a common understanding' (Bontis et al., 2002).

In summary: the format provided by a pattern provides a powerful way to capture and share knowledge in complex, knowledge intensive environments where it is impossible to make key aspects of knowledge fully explicit. This is the foundation for the concept and structure of the benefits toolkit.

The skilled professionals engaged in projects are not followers of rigid methods, but highly motivated 'craftsmen', passionate about the job, and skilled in using a range of tools, which they can adapt, based on experience to the specific situation they are facing.

First steps to a benefits-driven approach

Benefits review is a classic area where commons sense is far from common practice. It is also one of the best places to start with a benefits-driven approach. Carry out benefits reviews of recently completed and a few in-progress projects and see what you learn. Then make some targeted improvements and use the learning to plan broader adoption of benefits-driven ways of working.

Bridging the knowing-doing gap: building the benefits realization capability

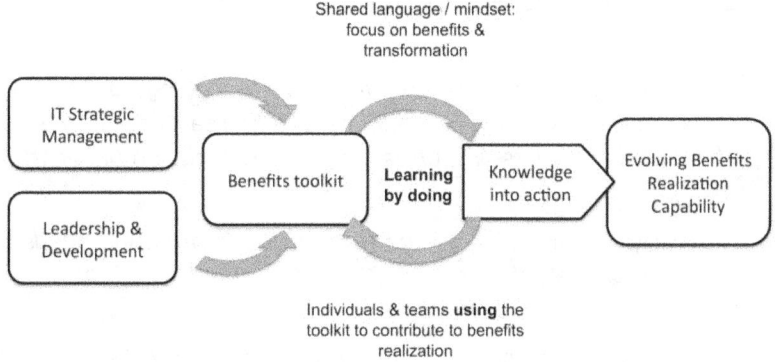

Figure 6.5: The toolkit contributes to putting knowledge into action to build the benefits realization capability of an organization.

***

7 Keeping moving: Expand

Key topics covered in this chapter:

o   *Most projects stop soon after new technology goes live. This is just when benefits start to be realized and this post-live phase requires a continued focus on benefits.*

o   *Exploitation of existing systems and information needs to become a priority.*

o   *Practices in this area are not yet well established, although some examples of good practice are starting to emerge.*

o   *In most organizations, there are good opportunities to increase benefits without any additional expenditure.*

Preparing for Expand

Expand goes beyond the end date of most projects – all too often, projects end at the technology live date plus 7 or 14 days. The team is disbanded and they move onto new projects or new customers just when they are needed most, just when everything they have learnt can really add value. Expand tackles the crucial post-live period when huge amounts of learning occur and when a continued focus on benefits realization is essential.

In our recent project, Exploring Business Transformation that involved 65 interviews with business and IT managers from a very wide range of organizations, we covered the area of Benefits Exploitation. Very often, it is left to chance: "*end users of systems lack knowledge – it's a case of loss of knowledge through staff turnover and passing on knowledge informally from one to the other*" (Business manager, financial services). The knowledge of what is possible and how to realize the full potential of the new technology is quickly fragmented and lost. When many organizations are still using systems 20 or more years old, this is an important area. This view was reinforced in our recent survey of senior business managers where exploitation of existing systems and information was the area of lowest satisfaction when we explored benefits from IT.

While handover to line or operational management will usually take place at this time, and service management disciplines will become important, we feel it is vital to consider Expand as part of the project. This makes planning for Expand a critical project activity and helps keep relevant members of the project team available during a transition period as benefits are established.

The issues will vary considerably from project to project. For example, in some infrastructure projects and branch deployment scenarios (retail, banking) much of the project effort may be after delivery of the IT solution.

Practices in this area of Expand are not yet well defined so for the moment we will share some ideas through a case study.

Expand: a case study

At Durham University, one of our major systems is referred to as DUO - Durham University Online. DUO is our eLearning environment and is used by all members of teaching staff and all students. DUO has a great many capabilities and can be used in many different ways to contribute to learning and the student experience. At a basic level, it is a way of making lecture notes available to students. At another level, it allows discussion groups, podcasts, wikis and interactive exercises. Which of these capabilities are used depends on the knowledge and interests of each member of staff and how they see DUO helping their students.

DUO is a good example of an IT system as a form of *intellectual* technology. DUO is an intellectual technology, not an *industrial* technology, in that it has properties that are not fixed on implementation, but can be innovated endlessly, depending on its interaction with the intellect of the human beings who use it. This can lead to an ongoing cycle of innovation and change as the technology extends the intellects of its users, leading to further innovation. This is a real challenge for many IT functions where the approach to projects is designed for an industrial technology – the way the system will be used is defined as part of the design and implementation. This approach might have worked for automating transactions but it is much less helpful when we use IT to help professional and knowledge workers.

At Durham, we have some good practices in place, which address the need for benefits exploitation – for continued learning and innovation. There is leadership for the usage and exploitation of DUO across the organization with support from a small, central team: "*our aim is to work with academic staff to help them enhance learning for students*". Responsibilities of the team include testing and releasing regular upgrades from the package suppliers, support and training for users, sharing good ideas and good practice. The team has a strong mixture of technical and business skills, in this case expertise in the design of eLearning.

The impact of these practices is to encourage gradual benefits exploitation as individuals and departments experiment and innovate, building on existing usage. This scale of investment is certainly not appropriate in every case, it is in this case as teaching and learning is the core business of the university. The example does demonstrate some good practices that can be adapted for different scenarios.

Examples of practices for Expand

A regular review of DUO usage, including an annual end-user survey, is carried out to understand satisfaction, identify problems and opportunities, and to provide input into future developments.

An annual user conference, which provides an opportunity for end-users to share how they are using the system and for good ideas to be communicated. The team provides additional input to the conference based on their work with the solution providers, and other organizations using the software.

Regular updates to help guides and training courses that address how to get the most value from the system. Help information is now provided in the form of a wiki, enabling broad participation in sharing ideas and advice.

Consultancy services to end-users, and user departments, with the aim of tackling specific projects to help them realize additional value from using the system: "we'll put in time to run a series of short seminars to provide updates on the new features and then we can work 1:1 with people who want specific advice".

Figure 7.1: Examples of practices for Expand

The **Benefits Review**[T] applies at this stage as at earlier stages of the lifeycle.

Implications for current projects

We initially tackle Expand when setting up the project, as the governance framework will establish key foundations. Specific areas to consider include:

- Inclusion of senior operational managers from the areas affected.

- Bringing members of key user areas into the project team.

- Ensuring the communications and stakeholder engagement strategy considers post-project roles and support for benefits exploitation.

- Using the training and deployment strategy to build expertise in key business areas and planning for key individuals to continue to play a role.

- Designing the system for ease of use and ease of training.

- Designing any help and training materials to make them easy to keep up to date.

One organization used the idea of a 'Benefits Assurance Team' to provide a post-live focus on building benefits realization.

Approach to benefits ramp-up: Benefits Assurance Team

The project had adopted the practice of 'phase benefits delivery'. It was decided to establish a Benefits Assurance Team combining Product Management and User Experience expertise. The Benefits Assurance team had a range of roles:

- Support for new ways of working – helping the operational management team 'bed in' the new ways of working and start to make improvements based on early learning.

- Monitoring the early results of benefits tracking and exploring options to realize and / or increase benefits.

- Following up the original training and making sure that staff were confident in both the systems and the ways of working.

- Working closely with operational management to ensure that they were able to manage the changed operations.

- Planning for the benefits realization review.

Figure 7.2: An approach to benefits ramp-up

Moving towards benefits exploitation

Active business leadership for benefits exploitation, along with the resources and relevant practices are vital aspects of an overall focus on benefits realization from IT. The story that 80% of the new features requested for Microsoft Office are already in the product, suggests that many users do not know the products very well and are not taking advantage of their potential. Office is far from unique in this respect.

In every organization we have worked with, there are major opportunities for action to increase the benefits realized from *existing* systems. Who is responsible for exploitation of benefits from each system in your organization? What are the good practices? How proactive is the role of the IT function? What if the role of the help desk shifted from responding to problems, to helping end-users realize benefits from the systems?

As with many other aspects of a benefits-driven approach, the key is just to make a start and to learn by doing:

- Review current projects and consider the effectiveness of arrangements for Expand.

- Review projects completed 12-18 months ago: what is the current position in terms of benefits realization? What additional opportunities are there?

- Carry out a benefits review of major systems or services including Microsoft Office and any major package applications (SAP etc). Think hard about how effectively the information and system capabilities are being used.

∗∗∗

8 Enabling innovation: adapting the approach

Key topics covered in this chapter:

- *IT is a critical enabler of business innovation.*

- *Business innovation to create new sources of value is a growing driver for investments in IT.*

- *A number of different perspectives can help provide insights into the opportunities for innovation.*

- *Insight into business and technology trends provides an important starting point for planning Exploratory investments.*

- *The agile, benefits-driven approach to IT-enabled change that we have presented is a good basis for innovation.*

- *Specific aspects of the approach can be emphasized to increase the chances of succeeding with innovation.*

Focus on innovation

Being more innovative is a key goal of many organizations. We feel it is right to make innovation a high priority given the business environment and the ongoing rapid innovation in IT.

Our key assumptions are that the continuing innovation in Information Technology is an important enabler of business innovation and transformation, and also that this IT innovation is not going to stop in the foreseeable future. Knowledgeable commentators, for example including Bill Gates, suggest that 'we ain't seen nothing yet' and the pace of innovation is likely to accelerate.

The challenge is to enable innovation to happen: to give it every possible encouragement, without creating unnecessary risks. Having established the foundations of a benefits-driven approach, a next step is to focus on projects and programmes of IT-enabled change to succeed with business innovation.

A key question is: what business opportunities do new and emerging technologies create? These might be new products and services, or significantly different ways of approaching existing activities. The focus remains on the business and benefits for stakeholders, this is not about technology for its own sake or technology research and development.

A key challenge for many CIOs and IT functions is: 'how can we be more effective at enabling business innovation and transformation?' In this section, we want to provide some context in terms of current IT trends and the potential impact on the business, and also consider some of the wider implications for the IT function and organization if it is going to succeed with IT-enabled business innovation.

Important note: This topic is important for all readers. A growing % of the investments in most organizations would benefit from taking advantage of an innovation perspective.

Innovation as a driver of value

The context for successful benefits realization

Organizations are trying to realize benefits from IT in a challenging environment. Some have argued that we are now operating in 'a new normal', involving high levels of uncertainty, and rapid and unpredictable change. We are also seeing 'digital natives' moving into the workforce and becoming more influential as customers. They certainly bring a new set of expectations: but will they be able to translate their ability to use technologies into benefits realization in the workplace?

There are many other factors to consider, not least the continuing rapid changes in technology and the delivery of technology based services, for example, as 'open source', 'cloud', 'software as a service' and mobile devices continue to have an impact. A key implication for benefits realization is the need to look outside the organization, to develop knowledge of trends and opportunities, and to invest time into building new capabilities.

Perspectives on innovation

'Innovation is the specific tool of entrepreneurs, the means by which they exploit change as an opportunity for a different business or service' (Peter Drucker, 1985). This does not limit entrepreneurs to the small business: innovation comes from entrepreneurial behavior in even the largest firms. Innovation does not require new technology, although it is often a factor.

Innovation strategies can be classified into the 4Ps: Product innovation, Process innovation (changing the way products and services are created or delivered), Position innovation (changing the context, for example the market, in which products and services are introduced) and Paradigm innovation (changing the underlying mental and business models which frame what an organization does) (Tidd et al., 2005 – see Figure 8.1). A second dimension is the degree of novelty involved. Is the innovation incremental, a change at the component level, doing something better? On the other hand, is it a radical innovation, a change at the system level, doing something new?

Definitions

Product innovation

Change in the way products or services are created or selected.

Process innovation

Change in the way products or services are delivered.

Paradigm innovation

Change in the underlying mental models which frame what an organization does.

Position innovation

Change in the context in which products and services are introduced.

Examples

Product innovation

Smartphone – mobile computing and communications not just voice.

Process innovation

Online retail banking.

Paradigm innovation

The phone 'app' market for Apple, Google, etc.

Position innovation

A small, regional UK business providing a global service without investing in an international sales team.

Figure 8.1: Innovation - definitions and examples

We explore a number of different perspectives on innovation to provide a foundation for exploring the issues in a specific scenario.

Technology adoption lifecycle

A widely used framework when exploring innovation is the technology or product adoption lifecycle (Figure 8.2). The model helps us think about the gradual adoption of a technology (or product or idea) into a marketplace.

The challenge is to develop innovative uses of technology and to create the customer demand to cross the chasm

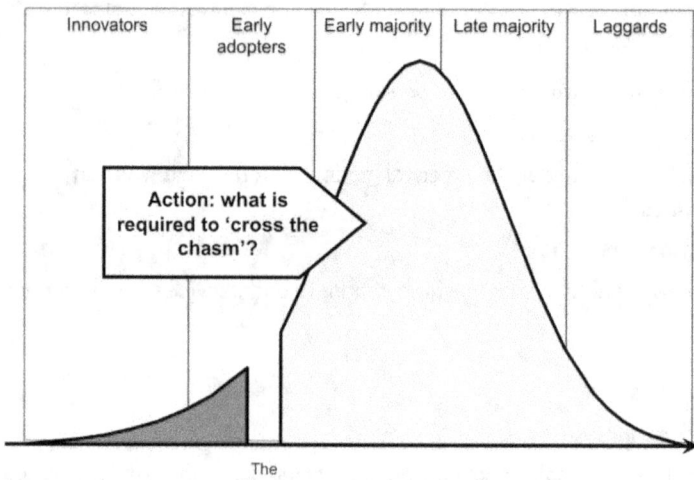

Figure 8.2: The technology adoption lifecycle

In Crossing the Chasm, Geoffrey Moore (1999) explores the characteristics of the different sections of the market and how to accelerate adoption. It is interesting to reflect the comparatively long adoption cycles associated with many 'new' technologies. I first came across RFID (Radio Frequency ID tags) over 15 years ago and it is still 'new' in many areas. Microsoft introduced tablet PCs in 2001 but mass-market appeal has only come with Apple's iPad in 2010.

In many cases, innovators have opportunities to use Exploratory projects to learn and build capabilities. A key decision is when to adopt early, taking into account that later adopters will still have to face some degree of learning curve to be able to exploit the opportunities.

Disruptive innovation

A second perspective is 'disruptive innovation'; where Clayton Christensen is the primary author. Disruptive technologies change the basis of competition: the memory stick has made the diskette obsolete, for example.

Disruptive innovation

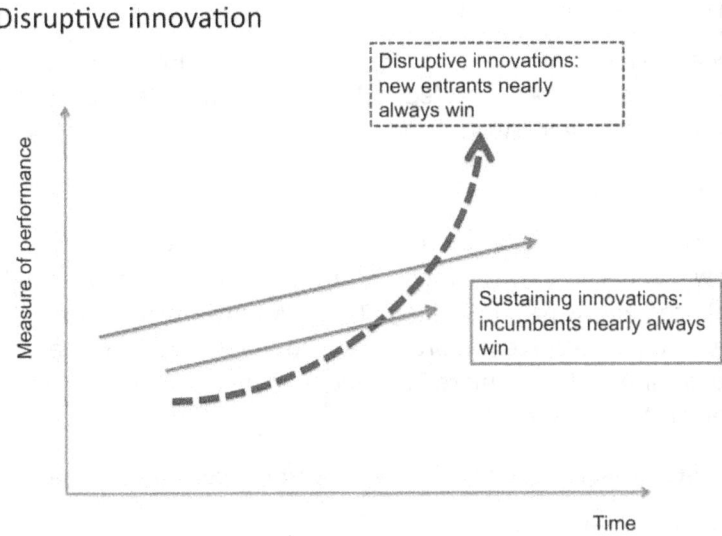

www.claytonchristensen.com

Figure 8.3: Disruptive innovation.

As Figure 8.3 indicates, in an established market, the incumbent usually has the economies of scale to improve price performance more quickly than new entrants. The opportunity for new entrants is to disrupt the market by introducing a new technology or tackling the problem in a new way. Incumbents often react much more slowly and are left behind as the new technology improves and gains broad adoption. The challenge, of course, is to have the vision to see the threat or opportunity.

Value innovation

A further angle is presented by Kim and Mauborgne in their book Blue Ocean Strategy (2005). They suggest that success and profitability come from 'value innovation'. Rather than fierce competition on price and performance in existing markets (red oceans), innovators see the world from a different perspective and create new market-spaces (blue oceans), with a different basis of competition. They give many examples, including a very simple mobile phone avoiding the race to add more features and functions and concentrating on ease of use for the large section of the market that still just want to make voice calls.

Blue Ocean Strategy also suggests that if the proposition is right it is possible to bypass the technology adoption cycle and go straight for the mass market.

Design thinking

'Design thinking' is about the *process* of innovation. It focuses on how people can work together to develop innovative products, services and ways of working. There is much in common with the agile, benefits-driven approach we have set out. There are many opportunities to do more to bring together the *design* and *agile* perspectives and toolkits.

Taking advantage of the different perspectives on innovation

The different perspectives on innovation can be valuable in: spotting opportunities; thinking through where to make investments; and approaching investments in a way that will increase the chances of success.

As a next step we explore some of the trends that are creating opportunities for business innovation.

The flat world: enabling business innovation

From automation and integration to innovation

Early uses of IT focused on automating and integrating existing processes, often replacing people with technology to enable great speed, scale and cost effectiveness. This is still a major driver for IT investments. Over the last decade, IT has increasingly become a driver and enabler of innovation in products, services and ways of working.

In his book, The World is Flat, Thomas Friedman discusses '10 Flatteners' that together have resulted in transformational change over the last 5-10 years. The only flattener that is not directly based on IT is the fall of the Berlin Wall. The outline in Wikipedia provides a good summary of the core argument. http://en.wikipedia.org/wiki/The_World_Is_Flat

The world is clearly not (yet) flat with billions still excluded by poverty. However, the core argument that the convergence of broadband, the PC, open standards, and powerful software has created huge challenges and opportunities is convincing. Friedman potentially underestimates the importance of social relationships and the power of inertia but it would be a risk to rely on these factors as insulation from the forces of change.

Friedman argues that the flat world crept up on us while we were asleep, distracted and depressed in the aftermath of the dot-com bubble and bust. In our exploration of benefits from innovation, it is important to consider our response to these flatteners and other IT based business and social trends. We can also consider what might be coming next, so we are not caught sleeping again. Scenario Planning is a valuable approach that provides a way to view the significant uncertainties involved in any longer-term forward planning.

Key trends – starting points for business innovation

This section provides a personal view of key trends. It is based on personal experience and reflecting on the views of many others. Clearly, we have no claim to have a better view of what is happening than anyone else and these ideas do not take into account wider technology developments (nano technology, quantum computing, etc).

Mobile computing. This is the 10th flattener. Increasing bandwidth, more reliable connectivity, and the power of new devices mean that new opportunities are emerging rapidly. We are moving to a situation where we have constant access to a full range of IT services and our own data across a wide range of devices. This is 'martini' computing: anytime, any place.

There are many challenges: security; work-home boundaries; and the digital divide, but there are also huge opportunities. In hindsight, we will probably see today as an experimental period where we were just starting to explore the potential of the tools available to us, and learning how to exploit them.

Enabling knowledge work. There is a lot of terminology to consider as different commentators talk about the knowledge economy and knowledge-intensive businesses. In essence, there is a switch in focus from using IT to *automate* transactions to using it to *informate* and contribute to the creativity and productivity of people. Many aspects of technology are relevant to the effectiveness of individuals, teams and organizations as they compete on adding value. Some of these technologies, for example related to collaboration and supporting virtual teams, have very broad application. Others are much more specialized. Friedman gives an example of how freely available software is changing the basis of competition in creative industries (artwork for advertising).

Again, many technologies are available but we have hardly begun to learn to exploit their potential.

Information management. New technology is providing organizations with vast stores of data; for example, the 'click stream' data of website usage or 'basket data' from retailer loyalty systems. The challenge is making use of this data to gain insight into how to create value for customers and to improve decision-making. Many tools, for example for data visualization, are becoming more widely available to help analysis and decision-making. At a more basic level, in many organizations there are many opportunities to get more out of widely available tools, such as Excel.

Cloud computing. We are using this as a broad term encompassing web services, software as a service and utility computing. These developments are making powerful, enterprise level software and scalable IT infrastructures available on a pay as you go basis. The open, Internet standards also mean that there are many opportunities for integration between systems and organizations. As a result, small organizations are much better placed to compete with large organizations, and large organizations have a range of new options to consider when planning how to supply their IT needs.

Challenges of innovation

There are a number of major challenges for organizations trying to make sense of these new developments and to identify where to make investments.

Pace of change: The pace of change is certainly high, but paradoxically many new developments have a long lead-time as they take years or even decades to go from a technical proof of concept to mainstream, cost effective, robust deployments. RFID is one example which enthusiasts were experimenting with in the mid 1990s but was only having an impact a decade later. Similarly we were working on projects to replace invoices with EDI 20 years ago, but organizations are still making major investments to scan invoices and introduce workflow software, so the invoice is nowhere near being eliminated.

Variety / uncertainty: Closely related are the issues of variety and uncertainty. In many areas (consider Web 2.0 technologies) there are very many competing products and services and it is far from clear which if any has a future and might emerge as a reliable, long term choice. IT departments have always faced this issue; perhaps today the extent of variety and the pace of change are greater.

Responding to the opportunities: enabling innovation

There are a number of areas we can build on the benefits-led approach to enable successful business innovation.

A portfolio perspective on innovation

Investments which *may* be important in achieving future success are **exploratory**. Often neglected, this is business R&D not technology experimentation. Exploratory projects can be about new products and services or new ways of working. They might involve adopting and adapting ideas from elsewhere. They are often about building new business capabilities through people, process and technology. Many knowledge management, customer relationship management and eLearning initiatives would have been good opportunities for Exploratory projects. There is clearly an opportunity – but the detail of how to realize it is not clear.

The starting point for innovation is to set aside some % of the budget and IT resources for investments in Exploratory projects. Small, high caliber teams need to be given small budgets and tight timescales to have a go and see what's possible. They won't all work – but some of them will provide valuable innovations that will lead to Strategic projects later on. Exploratory projects will also reduce the risks of much bigger failures – from launching into Strategic projects without really understanding what is possible or what customers and other stakeholders really want.

Exploratory projects require close engagement between senior business and IT managers. It is through this close relationship that the ideas emerge and opportunities are identified. They also require trust, a willingness to have a go, and the leadership to ensure that red tape does not stifle the innovation and learning at birth.

In essence, this is taking a venture capital or incubator approach. Small initial funding is topped up based on early success.

Project delivery – enabling innovation

Having spotted an opportunity and decided *where* to invest, the next challenge is to consider *how* to approach the project. Most approaches to IT projects are risk-averse and designed for an age when IT was mainly about automating well defined and well understood business processes. This is almost certainly not the case in an Exploratory project – by definition; you are doing something new. How effective will a waterfall approach to a project be, where you define the requirements in detail before going into a design stage? How effectively can you specify the requirements for something new and innovative before you go into design and development?

Exploratory projects are the ideal opportunity for following an agile approach and adopting relevant agile practices. An initial high-level vision and a small, multi-disciplinary team exploring what is possible replace upfront definitions of requirements. Key practices include:

Co-location: bringing the team members together so they can work together face to face with the minimum of paperwork. Their interaction will be the source of innovation

Multi-disciplinary team: ensure that key skills are in the team from day one, representing the organization, the customer and the technology possibilities.

Milestone based control – based on the idea of a 'timebox': tight timescales contribute to innovation. The team needs to work to clearly defined timescales, and stick to them, to ensure that the exploration and innovation does not drift. On Exploratory projects there should be a major milestone every 2-3 weeks. The focus on milestones keeps up momentum and motivation while avoiding too much micro-management. The key is to get a solution to the 'customer' and start learning.

Daily meetings: a 30-minute daily meeting might become the primary means of controlling the project and responding to problems and opportunities.

Agile approaches are not new. The Agile Manifesto was written in 2001 (www.agilemanifesto.org) and many of the principles and practices have been around for much longer. Why aren't more organizations adopting agile approaches, particularly for Exploratory projects?

Unfortunately, blame cultures and fear of failure get in the way of approaches that are more effective. It is safer to go by the book even if it's unlikely to result in real innovation.

For the entrepreneurial CIO, who is working closely with senior business colleagues, there is a real opportunity. Adopt the IT and Change portfolio, ring fence a small percentage of the IT budget for some Exploratory projects, build some small high caliber teams and let them have a go. Be ready to take responsibility if things go wrong on one or two, and recognize the efforts of the teams that succeed.

Strategic projects are critical to achieving strategic objectives. The goal is competitive advantage, a major shift in products and services or ways of working to create value for customers. They involve doing something new, often with the added pressure of the need for rapid results.

These major investments must be managed in a way that allows learning and innovation. Phased, incremental delivery is vital so that the learning is managed at a programme and portfolio level. At a project level it is often important to allow for exploration and learning, Traditional waterfall methods may not be a good fit.

Innovation – through Benefits Exploitation

'If all technological progress in the economy stopped today, would productivity growth grind to a halt? We don't think so. On the contrary, we believe that there are decades worth of potential innovations to be made in creatively combining (an making use of) inventions that we already have'

Brynjolfsson and Saunders, 2010; page 95

Innovation is not just about new technology and spending more money. What about all the technology we already have in place and have barely begun to exploit? Why not start with Word, the rest of Microsoft Office, SharePoint or even your ERP system? Without a doubt, you can quickly find some innovations that make a real difference to individuals, teams or your wider organization. Perhaps you can start a bigger process of building a climate where innovation happens. You might start by helping people discover some functionality that will make a real difference: surprisingly Styles, Table of Contents, Document Map in Word, Smart Art in PowerPoint, and using Outlook to set up meetings are still good starting points.

For most organizations, these opportunities just fall through the gaps between the Help Desk, which fixes problems, and the investment of technical skills in major projects. It is important to free up some resources to enable innovation when realizing benefits from existing IT investments.

Creating the environment for innovation

Beyond project and portfolio management there are many broader factors that contribute to an environment that enables innovation.

Learning by doing - building capability: In traditional IT projects the starting point is to prepare a detailed set of requirements and a business case, typically to automate an existing process, reducing costs and increasing speed. If the opportunity is for innovation, these approaches are a bad fit. From both business and IT perspectives, it is important to learn by doing – to explore how to add value and how to use the technology. The exploration is also building capability (knowledge and skills), so that if opportunities become Strategic the risks of major investment are much reduced.

Architectural approach: Paradoxically, an architectural approach to IT – establishing a coherent technical and application infrastructure may be an important enabler of innovation. It can ensure that the core infrastructure is robust and reliable and that there is good information integrity and depth of skills in key areas, which provides a platform for innovation around this foundation.

Shift the focus from governance to relationships: IT people like to talk about governance; we put a lot of effort into setting up structures and processes. It is important to remember that outside the IT bunker this is not how real organizations work, at least not at the top level. Too much focus on formal structures indicates the CIO is not part of the top team.

Governance structures are simply *a means to an end*: that is, getting the right people together to take decisions. It is far better to take a different approach and focus on building relationships – person to person. It is out of these relationships, not the IT governance committee, that innovation will grow.

From the wisdom of the leader to the wisdom of crowds: Is the CIO (or the CEO or any other leader) going to be one who has all the good ideas? No. We need to get much broader involvement in innovation. Our staff, customers, suppliers, competitors, perhaps even the local business school and university, should all be contributing.

The CIO needs to: go out and find the innovators and learn from their ideas; to provide opportunities for sharing ideas; and provide some (limited) resources to support people put their ideas into practice.

Implications for realizing benefits from innovation

There are places where too much innovation is a bad thing. Core Operations systems, for example, must not be put at risk. This means that the CIO and IT department, as a whole, needs to be able to adopt different approaches in different situations. This is certainly a challenge.

There are many other areas for action:

- Adoption of more agile approaches to projects.
- Adoption of the idea of Exploratory projects.
- Making small, staged investments in a range of opportunities. Investing further, as and when there is a clearer understanding of the potential.
- Emphasize learning by doing – so that prototypes and pilots can provide feedback and learning.

- Allocation of key technical resources to Exploratory projects and Exploitation activities.

- Emphasis on phased benefits delivery through a series of short projects.

- Building skills in collaborative, multi-disciplinary teamwork and effective stakeholder engagement.

- Exploring and taking advantage of the practices of 'design thinking.'

- Ensure that, as part of strategy and architecture activities, that there is a technology roadmap. This could, for example, look 1 and 3-5 years ahead at known and potential developments and provide a basis for planning exploratory investments and developing skills. The roadmap could be linked to the idea of the product adoption lifecycle.

- Taking proactive steps to facilitate the sharing of learning and opportunities across the organization and with key suppliers / partners.

Effective relationships between business and IT staff at all levels are critical if IT is to play its part as an enabler of business innovation.

***

9 First steps: adopting a benefits-driven approach

Key topics covered in this chapter:

- o *Adopting an agile, benefits-driven approach to projects is a programme of organizational change.*

- o *All that we have learnt about benefits-driven change applies to the challenge of gaining adoption of a benefits-driven approach to projects.*

- o *The programme of action required will vary by organization, although some core 'playbooks' (i.e. different approaches) are emerging.*

- o *There are usually a number of opportunities for 'quick wins.'*

Common sense?

This is all common sense? We hope so. We long for it to be common practice. If you think it is already common practice in your team or organization, just look slightly more carefully as there are very, very few places where that is the case. If you are still sure, please get in touch, as we would love to hear from you – it is great to learn from the success of others. If having looked you would like some help, still get in touch as we are passionate about helping individuals and organizations succeed in realizing benefits from IT-enabled innovation and change.

This chapter is about making it happen, about working out next steps for your project, team or organization and successfully introducing further aspects of a benefits-driven approach. We start by reflecting on the barriers to change, and then outline how to make improvements. We approach these improvements as a benefits-driven change programme and finally suggest some starting points.

Barriers to change

Recent research

We carried out a research project exploring the extent of adoption of benefits-driven practices. We studied more than 50 cases. The findings indicate that there is a very substantial gap between what we know from the literature about the impact of adopting a strong focus on realizing benefits through organizational change when managing IT projects, and what happens in practice.

The vast majority of the projects investigated for the study, focused on the design and delivery of an IT (technical) solution with only very limited coverage of the wider issues of work redesign, process re-engineering, organizational change management and benefits realization. We found no evidence of the adoption of a well-integrated portfolio of benefits realization practices and competences, which could be seen to demonstrate a *'benefits realization capability'*. Moreover, although we discovered many individual instances of specific practices being adopted, overall, these practices were not in widespread use, either within or across organizations.

Initial focus on benefits rapidly fades as projects progress

It was evident that the focus upon business benefits was most acute at a project's outset: most organization's attempted to identify the strategic drivers for their projects, and then establish the benefits that were sought. However, the rationale for adopting this approach owed more to getting the project authorized and funded, than it did to acting as a point of departure for the proactive management of benefits. Consequently, following their initial identification, business benefits tended to disappear from the project teams' agendas until the software was implemented, at which point the benefits might be evaluated, but rarely in a comprehensive or systematic fashion.

There was virtually no evidence to suggest that the project teams had actively engaged in the critical element of benefits realization, namely changes to the design of the organization, nor the re-engineering of business processes or the working practices of project stakeholders.

The only other significant stage at which business benefits were explicitly considered was during the post-implementation review, at which stage a number of project teams made clear recommendations that more specific benefits-related practices should be adopted in future projects. A number of teams noted that they had tried and failed to get their project sponsors to adopt benefits oriented practices.

Barriers to development of the benefits realization capability

In addition to discovering that there was remarkably little emphasis on benefits during the conduct of IT projects, our research also provides important insights into why the establishment of a *benefits realization capability* has, so far, been off the agenda for most organizations. It is a multi-faceted problem, but at its heart lie the twin problems of limited awareness of the possibility of different ways of working, and little appetite for moving away from their long established systems development approaches (Figure 9.1).

Reasons for the lack of adoption of benefits-driven approaches

A techno-centric mindset that places the delivery of technical solutions at the heart of all discussions.

Lack of awareness that benefits-driven approaches were available.

Misconception that benefits are already being addressed (for example, because a financial business case had been established).

Structural and cultural barriers to moving away from tried and tested systems development methods and approaches: resulting in lack of drive for change or failure of improvement efforts.

Structural and cultural barriers to changing the design of business processes and working practices, when implementing new software.

Inability to learn from previous experiences of poorly performing IT implementations.

Lack of (effective) executive sponsorship

Figure 9.1: Reasons for lack of adoption of a benefits-driven approach

Many organizations are in a 'mindset' where delivery of technology is seen as the objective of investments in IT. As a result, there is no drive for the adoption of benefits-driven approaches. These organizations are tending to adopt 'supply-side' solutions to the issues they see in realizing value from IT – these include off-shoring and outsourcing. From a benefits perspective this is tackling the wrong problem. The 'benefits realization capability' is 'hidden in plain view' and is not a focus for management.

Adoption as a change programme

One of the three in-depth case study organizations in our research was very successful in taking a benefits-driven approach to investments in IT. The projects we examined were part of a major Transformation Programme being carried out over a three-year period. In addition to the focus on realizing the intended benefits from the Transformation Programme the overall leader of the programme, and Transformation Programme team, were also working to develop the *benefits realization capability* of the organization. The aim was to develop an improved ability to tackle transformation and change, which would be of value beyond the initial three-year programme. In our terms, this transformation capability was a benefits realization capability. The organization is a strong example of successful benefits realization and provides valuable lessons as to what the benefits realization capability looks like and how to succeed in establishing it.

Adoption of a benefits-driven approach to IT-enabled change is itself a change programme, and often a very challenging one. Therefore, we need to apply what we have learnt about benefits-driven approaches to change to succeeding with this challenge. We need active business leadership, emphasis on engagement with stakeholders, a phased approach and a focus on benefits.

We focus on four areas: principles, process, practices and people.

Principles – a paradigm shift

The fundamental starting point is to recognize the real problem: that there is a need to develop a benefits realization capability. Adoption of benefits-focused approaches to IT is a 'paradigm shift' in perspective (mindset). As we saw at the other organizations in the research, the large majority of organizations act as if technology delivery is what makes a project successful

Making the shift to a real focus on benefits realization is potentially a significant challenge for individuals and organizations. The explicit principles that articulate the foundation of a benefits-driven approach help to enable this shift. The principles, for example, of "IT as an enabler" represent 'know-why', which is an important element in a major change programme. Without this paradigm shift there is a major risk that a benefits-driven approach will be adopted as yet another 'methodology' with no real change to attitudes and without the development of a new understanding. We saw this in another organization where the result was just painful compliance with yet another set of rules.

Individuals at the successful organization had a shared understanding that 'IT is an enabler' and that benefits come from a focus on the customer and other stakeholders. This underpinned their approach to projects, which became benefits realization through business change.

Process – common framework for benefits realization on projects

An overall framework or process for a benefits-driven approach is also required. From our research, a simple overall framework provides a structure for projects and the basis for a shared understanding and common approach. This is important as project teams are formed from across an organization and often across multiple organizations. Our e^{4+1} framework is a response to this need. The principles and process provide a starting point for a common language and effective teamwork.

This contrasted with other case study organizations where we found either no consistent approach to projects, or different approaches from different parts of the organization and from contractors resulting in confusion. It became hard for staff to get involved as their roles were not clear and projects became focused on technology delivery.

The successful organization was building this shared understanding of the process through providing education to all levels of managers to develop a common understanding of key elements of an approach to projects. This also reinforces the key principles. The education was backed up by the role of the leaders of the transformation programme who, through their involvement in planning and controlling the projects, helped establish a consistent approach.

Practices for benefits realization

The third element of the change programme is the phased adoption of improved *practices* for benefits realization. The successful organization we observed referred to this as a 'toolkit' and had linked the gradual introduction of new 'tools' with a programme of education and the provision of guidance and coaching from the transformation team to those learning how to apply them. In this book, we have provided important elements of a toolkit for benefits-driven IT-enabled change.

The toolkit approach makes it easy to learn and build skills gradually through incremental improvements. It also enables a flexible approach to the specific situation of each project and to match the skills of the people involved.

An important finding that emerged from the research is that a range of practices, for example risk management or phased delivery, can be applied to IT solution delivery or to a benefits realization project. The shift from solution delivery to benefits realization is subtle, for example affecting who is involved and the emphasis taken. For many practices, the shift from solution delivery to benefits realization is more about the new paradigm, or mindset, than a substantial change in the actual practice. There is a potential bonus that once the shift in perspective is made, a lot of what is already known is very valuable in the new paradigm.

Adopting a benefits-driven approach

Principles

The principles of a benefits-driven approach establish a new paradigm ('mindset').

Adherence to the new principles will require consistent and sustained communication from the leadership team. An education programme may be a very effective way to establish the principles and process and introduce key practices.

Process

An overall process or *framework* for a project establishes a common language and facilitates different groups working together.

In many cases, it will be possible to evolve a framework for a benefits-driven approach from existing approaches in use within an organization.

Practices

Many existing organizational practices will be valuable in the new 'benefits-driven' paradigm and other practices can be adopted from elsewhere (for example our evolving toolkit).

Phased development of a benefits focus for existing practices and adoption of a 'toolkit' of new practices for benefits realization contributes to the development of individual skills and organizational competences.

People

Underpinning everything are the skills of individuals and multi-disciplinary teams. The toolkit supports sharing of working practices and the building of 'craft' skills.

Figure 9.2: Adopting a benefits-led approach

People – developing 'craft' skills to succeed with benefits realization

Benefits realization requires high levels of skills from the people involved. As individuals and multi-disciplinary teams, they have to work effectively with each other and a very wide range of stakeholders.

The craftsman is passionate about the job. They are also expert in using their tools to get the job done. Their expertise takes time to develop. The expert's tools are often the same as those used by the novice but they can achieve much more.

The principles, process, and practices are designed to enable effective teamwork and engagement with stakeholders as project teams build a shared language and way of working. The tools are simple and common sense but they make a vital contribution to benefits realization.

Making a start

The goal is clear. The scope can be a specific project, projects within a team or across an organization. The starting point depends on you. It usually makes sense to start small, take a phased approach and learn by doing.

First steps might be to:

- Adopt a benefits-driven approach on one or two pilot project; and/or

- To carry out benefits reviews of a small number of recently completed projects.

One approach we have found valuable is to work with representatives from a number of project teams and a number of other stakeholders as a pilot group. We are just working with the IT Director, his management team and representatives from five projects and other influential individuals from within and outside IT on a programme of five one-day workshops spread over eight months. In the workshops, we are introducing elements of the benefits-driven toolkit, applying them there and then to the 5 projects. We are also working on skills for more effective stakeholder engagement and a more innovative, collaborative way of working.

It is important to see this as more than a quick win. The principles for benefits realization encapsulate a benefits 'mindset' which provides a crucial foundation for a benefits-driven approach to be successfully adopted. Developing this mindset will need sustained leadership.

Steps after the initial pilot(s) might include a benefits review of the overall project portfolio, wider education, and adoption on a second group of projects.

It makes sense to adapt the improvement programme to reflect the current context and build on existing strengths (see the examples).

Adopting a benefits-driven approach to IT projects: outline of a benefits plan

Drivers

- Increasingly competitive business environment. Product and service innovation, as well as cost reduction depend on IT.
- Currently the IT function is successful in delivering technology but less so engaging with the business areas to focus on benefits realization.

Objectives

- Establish a benefits-driven approach as 'business as usual.'
- Establish a culture of continuous improvement to develop the overall benefits realization capability.

Benefits

- Better selection of investment opportunities.
- Faster return on investment.
- Increased return on investment.
- Increased ability to innovate and create value in addition to cutting costs through IT.
- Increased staff energy and motivation.

Changes

- Follow a consistent project framework and use a common set of tools.
- Close business and IT working through multi-disciplinary teams

Enablers

- Education for project sponsors and teams.
- Support for pilot adopters of benefits-driven approaches.
- Clear business ownership for adoption of benefits-driven approaches.
- Regular review sessions to reflect on progress and drive learning and improvement.

Figure 9.3: Outline of a benefits plan for adopting a benefits-driven approach

Benefits Review

Carry out a benefits review of a small number of recently completed projects.

Benefits Review

Carry out a benefits review of a small number of ongoing projects.

Benefits Planning

Pilot a Benefits Planning process on 2-3 projects (i.e. Engage and Explore in terms of the e^{4+1} framework).

Consistent framework

Introduce e^{4+1} to provide a consistent framework for projects. Provide education aimed at specific audiences and work with key project teams to be sure they take on the framework successfully.

Figure 9.4: Starting points for adopting a benefits-driven approach

Looking ahead...

We have covered a lot of ground in this short book. Inevitably, there is more to say. We could explore how the approach applies when working with vendors or packages for example. A key area we have touched on, but not developed, is the skills required – of engaging with stakeholders, facilitating workshops and influencing others.

We are working on a second book, which will tackle a benefits-driven approach to strategy for transformation and change as well as management of the overall portfolio of investments in IT-enabled change and business innovation. These areas are also vital elements of the benefits realization capability.

***

Further Information

Further Reading

Strongly recommended: Ward, John and Daniel Elizabeth (2006) **Benefits Management**: delivering value from IS and IT investments. Wiley

***

Brown, John Seely. and Duguid Paul (2000) *The social life of information*. Harvard Business School (Chapter 4).

Checkland, Peter and Poulter, John (2006) *Learning for Action: A Short Definitive Account of Soft Systems*. Wiley.

Highsmith, Jim (2004) Agile Project Management. Addison-Wesley.

Kelley, Thomas (2001) *The art of innovation: Lessons in creativity from Ideo, America's leading design firm*. London: Harper Collins Business.

Kim, W.Chan and Mauborgne Renee (2005*) Blue Ocean Strategy*. Harvard Business School Press.

Manns, Mary Lynn and Rising Linda (2005) *Fearless Change: patterns for introducing new ideas*. Addison Wesley (Pearson Education).

Thorp, John (2003) *The information paradox: realizing the business benefits of information technology*. Toronto: McGraw-Hill Ryerson.

Wenger E., McDermott R. and Snyder W. (2002) *Cultivating communities of practice: a guide to managing knowledge*. Harvard Business School Press.

Friedman, T.L (2007) The World is Flat: The Globalized World in the Twenty-first Century. Penguin.

Software development and project management

McConnell, Steve. (1998) Software project survival guide. Microsoft Press

Coplien J and Harrison N (2005); Organizational Patterns for Agile Software Development; Pearson Prentice Hall

McCarthy, Jim. (1995) Dynamics of software development. Microsoft Press

Maguire, Steve (1998) *Debugging the development process: practical strategies for staying focused, hitting ship dates and building solid teams*. Microsoft Press

Boehm, Barry and Turner, Richard (2004*) Balancing agility and discipline: a guide for the perplexed*. Pearson Education

Avison, D. E. (1995) *Information systems development: methodologies, techniques, and tools.* McGraw-Hill, c1995

McManus John, and Wood-Harper Trevor (2003) *Information systems project management*. FT Prentice Hall

Design thinking

Brown, Tim (2009) Change by Design: How Design Thinking Creates New Alternatives for Business and Society: How Design Thinking Can Transform Organizations and Inspire. Collins Business

Kelley, Thomas (2001) The art of innovation: Lessons in creativity from IDEO, America's leading design firm. London: Harper Collins Business

Kelley, Tim (2008) The Ten Faces of Innovation: Strategies for Heightening Creativity. Profile Business

Martin, Roger (2009) Design of Business: Why Design Thinking is the Next Competitive Advantage. Harvard Business School Press

Innovation

Crossing the Chasm (1991, revised 1999) Geoffrey A. Moore

Christensen, Clayton M (1997) The innovator's dilemma: when new technologies cause great firms to fail. Harvard Business School Press

Christensen Clayton M. (2003) The innovator's solution: creating and sustaining successful growth. Harvard Business School Press.

Christensen, Clayton M. (2004) Seeing what's next: using the theories of innovation to predict industry change. Harvard Business School Press.

References

Alexander, C. (1977). A Pattern Language. New York: Oxford University Press.

Alvesson M and Karreman D (2001) Odd couple: making sense of the curious concept of knowledge management. *Journal of Management Studies*, 38(7) p995-1018.

Ambrosini V and Bowman C (2001) Tacit knowledge: some suggestions for operationalization. *Journal of Management Studies*, 38(6) p811-829.

Becker M (2001) Managing dispersed knowledge: organizational problems, managerial strategies, and their effectiveness. *Journal of Management Studies*, 38(7) p1037-1051.

Benjamin, R. and Levinson, E. (1993) A framework for managing IT-enabled change. *Sloan Management Review*. Summer 1993, 23-33

Bontis N, Crossman M and Hulland J (2002) Managing and organizational learning system by aligning stocks and flows. *Journal of Management Studies,* 39(4) p437-469.

Cash, et al. (1994), Building the Information Age Organization - building on Zuboff (1988); In the Age of the Smart Machine

Garvin, D.A. (1993) Building a Learning Organization. *Harvard Business Review*. July-August

Kamoche, K., Pina e Cunha, M. and Vieira da Cunha, J. (2003) Towards a theory of organizational improvisation: looking beyond the jazz metaphor. *Journal of Management Studies*, 40(8) p2023-2051.

McFarlan. F.W. (1981) Portfolio approach to information systems. *Harvard Business Review*, 59(5) p142-150.

Nandhakumar, J. and Avison, D. (1999) The fiction of methodological development: a field study of information systems. *Information Technology and People*, Vol 12(2).

Pfeffer, J. and Sutton, R. (1999) Knowing "What" to Do is Not Enough. *California Management Review*. Vol. 42(1).

Thompson and Walsham (2004) Placing knowledge management in context. *Journal of Management Studies*, 41(5) p725-747.

Tidd J., Bessant J. and Pavitt K. (2005) *Managing Innovation: Integrating technological, market and organizational change* (Third edition). Chichester, West Sussex. John Wiley and Sons Ltd.

Treacy, M. and Wiersema, F. (1993) Customer Intimacy and Other Value Disciplines. *Harvard Business Review*, Jan-Feb

Appendix: The Toolkit

The toolkit concept provides a general framework for capturing lessons learned and knowledge that might otherwise remain tacit and very hard to share. It provides a flexible body of knowledge that individuals and teams adapt as they tackle different situations.

The 'tools' in the toolkit are an effective way to capture and share knowledge in challenging situations where the answers are not always clear.

Our benefits realization toolkit draws on many years of accumulated experience of leadership and the strategic management of IT. The programme to build the benefits realization capability of an organization has many elements: phased adoption of a toolkit of practices for benefits realization is a vital element.

***

www.ingramcontent.com/pod-product-compliance
Lightning Source LLC
Chambersburg PA
CBHW081121170526
45165CB00008B/2514